CW00469564

Practical Be Management for Primary School Teachers

Tracey Lawrence

B L O O M S B U R Y
LONDON • OXFORD • NEW YORK • NEW DELHI • SYDNEY

Bloomsbury Education
An imprint of Bloomsbury Publishing Plc

50 Bedford Square
London
WC1B 3DP
UK

1385 Broadway
New York
NY 10018
USA

www.bloomsbury.com

BLOOMSBURY and the Diana logo are trademarks of Bloomsbury Publishing Plc

First published in Great Britain 2017

A catalogue record for this book is available from the British Library.

ISBN
PB 9781472942357
ePub 9781472942333
ePDF 9781472942364

2 4 6 8 10 9 7 5 3 1

Typeset by Newgen Knowledge Works Pvt. Ltd., Chennai, India
Printed and bound by CPI Group (UK) Ltd, Croydon, CR0 4YY

This book is produced using paper that is made from wood grown in managed, sustainable forests. It is natural, renewable and recyclable. The logging and manufacturing processes conform to the environmental regulations of the country of origin.

To find out more about our authors and books visit www.bloomsbury.com. Here you will find extracts, author interviews, details of forthcoming events and the option to sign up for our newsletters.

This book is dedicated to Amy and the Lawrences, who support me unconditionally and enable me to be the best teacher that I can be.

To all of the children, parents, teachers and colleagues that I have met throughout my time in teaching: thank you, for in some way you will have supported, challenged and inspired my thinking.

Contents

Contents

Acknowledgements

I am ever so lucky to have a fantastic network of people that are happy to freely share their thoughts, ideas and strategies used. Inspiration for this book came from too many places to mention, including my colleagues on #behaviourchat and via Facebook. Also, each and every child and parent that I have worked with – I've really valued those connections. Not only have I been able to support them through difficult situations but I have also had that support back from them, through the most challenging two years that I have faced. For that, I am eternally grateful.

There are a few people that I would like to acknowledge individually. To Debbie Palphreyman (@elsasupport), who has been an endless source of support and is able to provide such an insight into the emotional development of children, thank you. To Cherryl Drabble (@cherrylkd) and Lynn McCann (@reachoutASC), who have talked to me throughout the whole process and supported me, thank you. To Mark Oldman (@moldman83), who has provided support, particularly with reference to the behaviour for learning driving licence, thank you.

A final thank you to Miriam Davey, who has been an inspiration and a huge support in getting this book put together. From the very first day when I realised that we had the same vision for children, I knew that we would be an amazing team. And we were. Thank you!

How to use this book

There are a variety of attitudes towards behaviour management. You may already have met the attitude that children with social, emotional and mental health needs (SEMH) should either be dealt with by specialists or removed from mainstream settings. As a class teacher, you are responsible for the progress of all the children in your class and in buying this book, you will come to understand the different areas of behaviour and have some ways forward.

We will bust some jargon for you, enabling you to feel more confident when dealing with these different areas, and you will be able to continually improve your practice as a teacher for the different children that walk through your classroom door year on year.

You don't need to read this book in any particular order. Each chapter acts as a 'dip in, dip out' guide to suit the variety in children's behaviour. It will offer different levels of strategies to support you in your experience and individual journey. In each chapter, you will meet useful background information, practical strategies that can be taken straight into the classroom, opportunities for reflection and even online resources. There are case studies that show you real-life situations within a classroom, as well as tried-and-tested methods to implement in these specific situations. There are different levels of strategies, dependent on both your current level of confidence and things that you may have tried already.

Chapter 1 – in this chapter, you will meet a jargon-buster straight away to support your understanding, followed by a discussion on different theories of behaviour, providing you with deeper knowledge on what behaviours may present themselves in your classroom.

Chapter 2 – this chapter explains what is meant by low-level behaviour and how you can eliminate this within the classroom as well as encourage positive learning behaviours. It will provide you with some online resources that will support you in this.

Chapter 3 – this chapter will link into behaviour for learning within your classroom. It will support you in identifying passive behaviour and motivating those disengaged children. Through ideas and strategies, you will be able to build character traits and enable your children to start looking after their own learning.

Chapter 4 – this chapter will cover the different behaviours that may be considered extreme within a mainstream primary school, including behaviour arising as a result of special educational needs and disabilities (SEND). It will support you in writing behaviour plans and in looking at alternative provision, if needed.

Chapter 5 – this chapter looks at mental health and causes for different behaviours presented. It covers areas such as attachment, bereavement, trauma and others. We look at emotional literacy and how this can be placed into your classroom to support your vulnerable children.

Chapter 6 – this chapter will provide you with strategies to support children's well-being as well as the well-being of yourself and your colleagues. It will allow you to develop your anxiety toolkit, promoting calming strategies for you and the children. It will also look at different initiatives that promote positive well-being.

Chapter 7 – this chapter provides you with a wealth of different interventions that you could use straight away with your children. There are links to online resources you can use immediately to support your children and enable them to be ready for learning.

Chapter 8 – this chapter will look at developing relationships with your children and your team. It will deepen your knowledge of questioning and how you can use this with your children. Within the chapter, we look at behaviour scripts that can ensure consistency within your team. It will also support you in developing relationships with parents.

Chapter 9 – this chapter looks at assessing children with SEMH in the mainstream classroom. We will cover different forms of assessments that will enable you to show progress with your children, even if this cannot be measured academically. It will support you when it comes to reporting about the 'whole child' and will move away from just measuring academic attainment.

Chapter 10 – this chapter looks at continuing professional development (CPD), which can have a high impact as well as being cost-effective. It will show you how social media and networking can support you with the challenges that behaviour can bring to a mainstream classroom.

So, what are you waiting for? Dip in and remember to share the things that you learn with your colleagues, whether it is through informal networking in the staffroom or via the #behaviourchat hashtag on Twitter.

Make sure you Tweet photos of you reading your copy of the book and use the hashtag on Twitter or join us on Facebook to discuss anything further. There's a network out there ready to support you in your classroom.

Online Resources accompany this book at:
www.bloomsbury.com/primary-practical-behaviour-management
Please type the URL into your web browser and follow the instructions to access the resources. If you experience any problems, please contact Bloomsbury at: companionwebsite@ bloomsbury.com

Preface

Teaching and supporting a child with SEMH difficulties can be extremely draining. However, those moments when you see your child engaging in learning, working with another child and beginning to develop a relationship with you are so worthwhile. It's at that point that you can begin your journey of discovering new concepts, embracing curiosity and having an impact on the well-being of that child.

You may have people offering to throw magic wands of behaviour management at you. This is a frustration that we will power through. There is no magic wand. No single strategy will enable all SEMH children to achieve. There is, however, a journey – a journey towards ensuring that *all* children within your classroom *can* and *will* achieve.

The purpose of this book is to build your knowledge of the possible background factors that indicate why children behave in the way that they do, as well as offering different layers of strategies that you will be able to try within your own classroom. It will also offer you the opportunity to think about, reflect on and question your own practice and the impact that it has on the progress of your children.

This book will provide you with tried-and-tested practical strategies that will support you in your behaviour management. It will build upon strategies to support you in dealing with the low-level behaviour challenges that you will face, as well as help you with the extreme behaviours that you may face within a mainstream classroom. I hope that, when reading this book, you will unlock the confidence within yourself to discover strategies that will suit your own style of teaching and that will, in turn, support your SEMH children to achieve and progress.

Chapter 1
What is behaviour?

There is a fear when talking about behaviour – fear of looking incompetent. I've sat in meetings, nodded and smiled at acronyms that I didn't know through fear of looking inept and unintelligent.

Let's solve that now. Here is a list of acronyms that you may come across in the area of behaviour and which you may hear in meetings, discussions and even this book. Not only will I provide clear and simple definitions of the acronyms, but I will also explore the term 'behaviour' and how it differs from setting to setting, as well as government opinions. I will relate this to your own classroom setting as well as directing you to chapters that will be useful for you to read straight away.

Jargon-buster

ADHD/ADD	Attention Deficit (Hyperactivity) Disorder
ASD	Autistic Spectrum Disorder
BESD	Behavioural, Emotional and Social Difficulties; when looking at behaviour prior to the SEND Code of Practice 2014, this was the acronym that was used in relation to children struggling with their behaviour.
CAF	Common Assessment Framework
CAMHS	Child and Adolescent Mental Health Service
EHA	Early Help Assessment
EHCP	Education, Health and Care Plan; this replaced the statement in the SEND Code of Practice 2014. It allows children with needs to access specialist provision.
EP	Educational Psychologist
EWO	Education Welfare Officer

IBP	Individual Behaviour Plan; this can also be referred to as BEP – Behaviour Education Plan. You may also see this referred to as PSP – Pastoral Support Plan.
LAC	Looked After Child
ODD	Oppositional Defiance Disorder
PDA	Pathological Demand Avoidance
PEP	Personal Education Plan; this is a document that is completed, usually termly, for children that are currently in care.
PHP	Personal Handling Plan
PRU	Pupil Referral Unit; this is the provision that a child goes to when they are excluded from mainstream school.
RA	Risk Assessment
SEMH	Social, Emotional and Mental Health; this is the 'label' that came out of the SEND Code of Practice in 2014. It replaced the label of BESD.
SEND	Special Educational Needs and Disabilities
SENDCo	Special Educational Needs and Disabilities Coordinator
SpLD	Specific Learning Difficulties
TAC	Team Around the Child; this is a meeting that will be called with all relevant professionals who have the child in common. It will allow you to think strategically about how to support your child. You may also know this as a MAST, which is a Multi-Agency Support Team.
YISP	Youth Inclusion Support Panel

When you're in these meetings and floored by the introduction of a new acronym, scribble it down and find it out at a later date or ask somebody that you feel comfortable with, but don't ignore it.

So... back to 'What is behaviour?'. According to the Oxford Dictionary, it is 'the way in which one acts or conducts oneself, especially towards others'. My idea of behaviour could be totally different to yours. Our experiences could be poles apart but with the commonality of a definition. If our ideas vary, then they will vary to other colleagues, our senior leadership team (SLT), the parents of children within our class and the children themselves. 'Difficult behaviour' to us may be viewed as 'acceptable behaviour' at home and vice versa. It is important to keep this in your mind when thinking about behaviour, especially when trying to rationalise reasons.

I surveyed social media for different ideas on what behaviour is, and here's what I found:

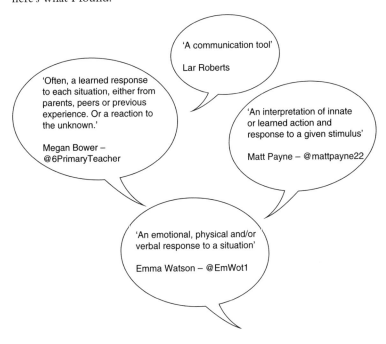

'A communication tool'

Lar Roberts

'Often, a learned response to each situation, either from parents, peers or previous experience. Or a reaction to the unknown.'

Megan Bower – @6PrimaryTeacher

'An interpretation of innate or learned action and response to a given stimulus'

Matt Payne – @mattpayne22

'An emotional, physical and/or verbal response to a situation'

Emma Watson – @EmWot1

The Association of Teachers and Lecturers (ATL) surveyed teachers in 2015, and trainee teachers that had considered leaving the profession cited behaviour as being one of the top five reasons for doing so. That won't be us. We will identify behaviours, have strategies to support those children, and allow our children to regulate their behaviour and then progress within their learning.

In the jargon-buster on page 1, I mentioned the change in category from BESD to SEMH in the SEND Code of Practice 2014. The Code of Practice clearly outlined that, as a teacher, you need to identify whether the behaviour that your child is exhibiting is a result of SEND or not.

'Children and young people may experience a wide range of social and emotional difficulties which manifest themselves in many ways. These may include becoming withdrawn or isolated, as well as displaying challenging, disruptive or disturbing behaviour. These behaviours may reflect underlying mental health difficulties such as anxiety or depression, self-harming, substance misuse, eating disorders or physical symptoms that are medically unexplained. Other children and young people may have disorders such as attention deficit disorder, attention deficit hyperactive disorder or attachment disorder.'

(SEND Code of Practice, 2014)

With budget cuts having a huge impact on provision for our children, behaviour support has been dwindling rapidly. The new curriculum expectations and assessment frameworks have put more emphasis on higher standards of academic assessments, resulting in more pressures on our children to achieve. The differentiation between behaviour as a result of SEND and children displaying disruptive behaviour has shown us two different ways of assessing. As outlined in the Rochford Review, if the behaviour is a result of SEND, then your school can decide on the form of assessment that is appropriate. However, if behaviour is not a result of SEND, then the assessment framework still applies. Chapter 9 will support you in showing different forms of progress that may not be linked to academic attainment.

With the SEND Code of Practice came more recognition for the behaviours that teachers are dealing with within a mainstream setting. Guidance was released on looking at 'Behaviour and Discipline within Schools' which gave teachers more power with respect to the following:

- Having the power to discipline pupils in school – and, in some circumstances, this can be extended to outside of school.

- This responsibility extends to all paid staff, including your TAs, dining supervisors, etc., so the team around the child can be larger and more consistent.

- Setting your rewards and consequences policy, allowing for a more effective and consistent approach within school.

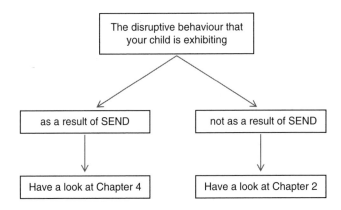

Schools and colleges should have clear processes to support children and young people, including how they will manage the effect of any disruptive behaviour so that it does not adversely affect other pupils.

Behaviour is like an umbrella, with a variety of different diagnoses sitting underneath it. You might recognise some of them, as they may appear within either your classroom or the whole school.

Attention Deficit Hyperactivity Disorder (ADHD)

There are two main strands within ADHD:

1. Inattentiveness

2. Hyperactivity and impulsiveness

Children with ADHD generally have problems that fall into both of these categories, but this isn't always the case so you may hear of other terminology as well. Some children don't have any problems with hyperactivity nor impulsiveness, and only have difficulties with inattentiveness. In this case, rather than being diagnosed with ADHD, they are instead diagnosed with Attention Deficit Disorder (ADD). These symptoms may be less obvious, so sometimes go unnoticed within your classroom.

Anxiety

Anxiety can present in either a mild or severe form. It is a feeling of unease, often pinpointed as worry, fear or apprehension. Feeling anxious can be perfectly normal during times where it is expected – for example, before a Christmas production or during exam times. Some children find it hard to control their worries, so their feelings of anxiety happen in daily life where these bigger activities aren't actually present. Anxiety is the main symptom of several different conditions, including panic disorder, phobias, post-traumatic stress disorder (PTSD) and social anxiety disorder. You may hear about generalised anxiety disorder (GAD), which is a long-term condition that causes you to feel anxious about a wide range of situations rather than one specific event. Children with GAD feel anxious most days, and once an anxious thought is alleviated, it is replaced with another. Symptoms can include feeling restless or worried, having trouble concentrating or sleeping and dizziness or heart palpitations.

Oppositional Defiant Disorder (ODD)

ODD is defined by negative and disruptive behaviour, particularly towards authority figures, such as parents and teachers. It is estimated that between 2% and 16% of children have ODD, and it is more likely to be identified in boys. It typically begins by eight years old, although cases of ODD being diagnosed in mainstream primary schools are rare.

The cause of ODD is not currently known but it is believed that it is a combination of three factors that may contribute to the condition: biological, genetic and environmental.

Biological

Some studies suggest that defects to certain areas of the brain, as well as injuries to these areas, can lead to serious behavioural problems. ODD has also been linked to high amounts of special chemicals in the brain. Symptoms of ODD have been identified when chemicals are out of balance or not working properly. Often when children have ODD, they have other mental health difficulties such as ADHD, other learning difficulties, depression and anxiety disorders.

Genetics

There is a suggestion that a vulnerability to developing ODD may be inherited. Many children with ODD have close family members with mental health conditions, including mood disorders, anxiety disorders and personality disorders.

Environmental

It is also suggested that a dysfunctional family life, substance use and inconsistent discipline may contribute to the development of ODD.

Symptoms of ODD may include:

- throwing repeated temper tantrums
- excessively arguing with adults
- actively refusing to comply with requests and rules
- deliberately trying to annoy or upset others, or being easily annoyed by others
- blaming others for your mistakes
- having frequent outbursts of anger and resentment
- being spiteful and seeking revenge
- swearing or using obscene language
- saying mean and hateful things when upset.

Conduct Disorder

This often involves a tendency towards highly antisocial behaviour, such as stealing, fighting, vandalism and harming people and/or animals.

So here we go... let's start our journey picking apart behaviour, looking at the underlying causes of behaviour and working together to have a positive impact on your classroom and achieve the best outcomes for our young people.

Chapter 2
Low-level behaviour

Our government stated that the impact of low-level behaviour equates to 38 days of lost education for children each year. This equates to over a year of their education wasted because of low-level behaviour. In this chapter, I will support you in going through different stages of low-level behaviour and describe how to manage this within your classroom, providing all of your children with a better atmosphere for learning. Managing the low-level behaviour will reduce escalation. Escalation into high-level behaviours will negatively impact on your classroom, but these low-level behaviours can be unpicked and channelled into positive learning behaviours.

What is low-level behaviour?

Similar to our differing definitions of behaviour in general, low-level behaviours are also different in that I could reel off several low-level behaviours that I have experienced within my classroom, none of which apply to your setting. Therefore, let's use a tool that will enable you to not only identify these behaviours but prioritise them into an action plan of reduction:

Diamond 9 (see **Online Resources**)

1. Using nine sticky notes, write a low-level behaviour on each that you have experienced within your classroom.
2. Use them to form a diamond, with the most regularly experienced low-level behaviour at the top of the diamond.

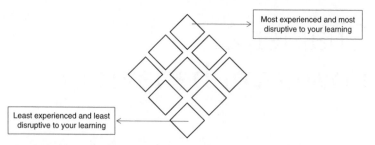

Most experienced and most disruptive to your learning

Least experienced and least disruptive to your learning

3. Bear in mind that these behaviours can and will change. You may also feel that all nine are equally important but, in order to tackle this effectively, you will need to take the emotion out of the behaviour and prioritise it.

4. Discuss your choices with another member of staff, just to have that dialogue, but remember that this is your classroom and it is your choice as to what the order is.

5. Look at the low-level behaviour that appears at the top of your Diamond 9. Then think about an action plan for tackling only that behaviour.

> **Top Tip:** *Make sure change is implemented before you go to the next level of review.*

Shouting out

The following case studies will provide you with a real-life situation from a primary school, describing the behaviours that were presented and providing you with strategies to implement.

> ### Case study: Nicola – aged nine
>
> Nicola is a nine-year-old girl. She is a high achiever who is popular with the other children in the class. She engages in your lessons and is keen to contribute. However, she regularly shouts out during input and with questioning. She wants to answer a question before anybody else and appears to have no awareness for others in a lesson.

As a teacher, this is draining, as you deal with this regular interruption to your lesson and others' learning.

If you have a similar child in your class, you need to identify the following:

Question 1: Is your child shouting out in order to contribute to your lesson? If yes, move on to the practical strategies.

Question 2: Is your child shouting out through choice and does it seem like they are trying to gain attention within the class and/or to cause disruption? If yes, move on to the next case study.

Practical strategies to support Nicola

1 – Positive behaviour-spotting

Nicola is eager to please. Build on this. Spot and comment on the behaviour that you want to encourage. Be specific in your praise – for example, 'Ooh, Lisa is sitting so well in her chair. I can't believe how straight you are sitting!'. This will tap into your children's desire to please you. Suddenly, your children will sit up nicely/put their hands up to answer a question and show the desired behaviours without you having to reprimand for undesired behaviours.

Take this a step further: As you spot the bubbling behaviours within Nicola, you will be able to notice her become fidgety, struggling to contain her over-excitement in answering questions. Here is where you can start praising the behaviours that you want to see in your classroom. At this point, those behaviours that you are trying to decrease haven't even entered your classroom and you are becoming more proactive in your approach! Well done, you!

2 – Your presence within the classroom

Nicola is looking for your recognition. She wants to get the answer right and she wants to engage in your lesson, whilst actually causing a disruption to others' progress. As you are working with a class of nine to ten year olds, you can usually allow children to be at their tables during input. This is the perfect setting for capitalising on your presence and Nicola's need for recognition. Circle the room whilst you're completing your input, and join in with groups when you are throwing out open questions to get partners discussing. When you see Nicola 'calling out', head over and simply put your hand on her shoulder. It's a small recognition that you know she's there and you value her response but it also acts as a reminder to her that she needs to put her hand up and/or wait her turn.

> **Take this a step further:** *Invest in a clicker or use ICT to enhance your presence, by being able to share work and continue your teaching input from anywhere in the room. You will be able to monitor the progress of all children and support where necessary with behaviour. Again, you're acting in a more proactive way.*

3 – Active teaching

Ensure that there are active elements to your lesson to keep it fast-paced and engaging. Not every lesson can be 'all singing and all dancing' but you can ensure that you have those active elements there to engage all children, including Nicola. Check your use of the following:

- Talk partners – allowing children to talk to their partner about their learning brings that opportunity to discuss the learning with another. It will either help to consolidate learning or they can get support from peers.

- Activities – opportunities to complete a mini-activity based around the children's learning.

- Questioning – by teachers questioning the children through the use of open and closed questions, you again provide the opportunity for talk to engage learners and probe understanding.

- ICT – can you use online resources to engage and provide a break for the children in your class?

- Outdoor provision – physical approaches to learning will support learners in their engagement.

There are many other ways of engaging and providing active learning within your lessons, so plan for them and engage all, including Nicola.

Take this a step further: Get the children involved in planning their own learning. Can they tell you what they want to learn about in their topic? Can they plan their own learning approaches? Once you eliminate that low-level behaviour, your opportunities for enriching learning are endless.

Here is another case study from a slightly younger child, exhibiting differing behaviours that would also be classed as shouting out. I will share these behaviours and provide you with practical strategies for immediate implementation.

Case study: James – aged eight

James is an eight-year-old boy. He seems popular with the other boys in the class but doesn't have a firm best friend. He shouts out randomly during lessons. This isn't always on topic, although it can be. It will usually be a quip, a joke at your expense or something designed to make others laugh. This behaviour interrupts your flow of teaching, distracts others' learning and causes you frustration and aggravation.

James is the child that appears to be able to choose his behaviour. We haven't delved further into his behaviour but, for this example, we are looking at it on a superficial level of **choice**. James is choosing this behaviour and needs a different approach.

Practical strategies to support James

1 – Discussions

James is eight years old and previous teachers and school staff will have tried and tested strategies to deal with his behaviour. Write them down under a list of successful and not successful strategies, and then implement the successful strategies – but not all at once. Try one and give it a chance to embed in your classroom routine. Ensure that all staff and volunteers are aware of the strategy that you will employ so that consistency is available.

Question: Has James' low-level behaviour been present in previous years or has it just begun this year?

If James' behaviour has only begun this year, then you need to question why. Discussions are extremely important in this case. Speak to your SENDCo; have there ever been any causes for concern? Speak to other adults that cover your class and work in your class; are they experiencing the same thing? Speak to James' parents/carers; have there been any changes at home that you need to be aware of and/or support?

Tips on having conversations with parents about behaviour

- First and foremost, you are talking about their child. Don't forget that, although you may be able to separate their child from their child's behaviour, parents are still connecting the two. When you discuss negative behaviour, be mindful that they may see this as a direct insult about their child and, in turn, their parenting.

- Don't focus on the negatives. By the time you have the conversation, it would be easy to launch into a tirade of what their child has done wrong, but remember that this child is just that – a child. There are also positives that you can pull out to ensure that a parent doesn't leave the discussion feeling awful about their child and themselves as a parent.

- Build relationships early. Make yourself visible. Say hello every morning, smile and be aware of how approachable you are. In this case, where you are going to need to have what could be perceived as a difficult conversation, you will have built up the most basic of relationships, which will allow for an open conversation. Don't underestimate the length of time and emotional investment you will have with this family. It's vital that the relationship is positive from the beginning.

- Respect parents' relationships on the playground. Don't go over to a parent while they are standing with a group of their peers and ask for a conversation or, even worse, start having the conversation then and there. All you will do is encourage

---

defensive or aggressive behaviours. Call the parents ten minutes before the end of the day and ask them to come and meet you to have your discussion. You can have a private conversation and no one has to feel any embarrassment or feel fearful about it.

- Be aware of family dynamics. If you are dealing with a family where the parents are separated, call both of them, as both parents will be involved in the child's life, even if it doesn't appear that way. You will need to have consistency in messages given out to parents. Don't rely on parents speaking to each other and passing on messages. It can cause blurry paths of communication at best.

- Avoid jargon and too much information. As a teacher, you will be delving deeper behind the scenes. Parents do not need to know this straight away. Avoid panic. The first conversation needs to be short and to establish your role as a team. Make them aware that you both have the child's best interests at heart and, rather than asking them to 'deal with the problem', explain that you are working together to support the child in the best way that you can.

2 – Communication

Use the following lines of communication to support James' behaviour. Sometimes children's behaviour can be supported simply by all lines being open for communication, and therefore all being aware of what is happening day in and day out.

- Email – make sure that you use your work email in order to protect yourself. Also, keep copies of emails for reference and to pass on to future colleagues.

- Home-school communication book – designed to be a brief communication tool detailing the day's events at home and at school. Importantly, don't let this turn into a 'moan book' – include positives, learning that has happened at school, etc. If it just has the bad points of the day in it, then the child will view it as 'the enemy' and it is less likely to make it home.

- Behaviour chart (see **Online Resources**) – a behaviour chart can simply be a method of communication, sharing how the day has gone. It can break the day up into smaller chunks that are achievable. It gives you discreet opportunities to coach the child and focus them on the targets. Avoid making a show of this; it should be genuine praise in response to a child meeting their behaviour target, **not** a reward for things that they find easy.

Take this a step further: With children aged seven and above, allow them to identify their own behaviour targets to focus on. Ask them how they would like these to be communicated to parents and who they would like to be told. They may surprise you when they ask you to make a positive phone call to Grandma instead of the person picking up day in and day out. It has to be meaningful for the child.

3 – Activities

When you have a child struggling with particular aspects, like James does, then you may need to think about providing support via intervention. You can focus on the specific aspect that needs work. In James' case, this would be his shouting out. Plan it in the same way that you would plan any intervention: assess, plan, do and review.

1. Assess the need – in James' case, through observation in class and/or any tracking, it will be apparent that James needs support in working on reducing his incidents of shouting out.

2. Plan – a six-to-eight-week intervention that fits in with other interventions that are happening in class.

3. Do – an activity that you could do during this intervention time is discussing an incident that may have happened that week. Discuss the following:

   - Where were you when the incident of shouting out happened?
   - What did you say and in response to what?
   - What did your teacher say? Why do you think they said that?
   - Did you stop or did you continue?
   - What was the consequence?

You could then use the behaviour script online resource (see **Online Resources**) to stage an alternative conversation. Discuss the response that James could have given and discuss explicitly the choices that he had to avoid the consequence that he received.

4. Review each session – an extremely useful way of reviewing engagement is to measure it against a colour-coding system, with red meaning that there was no engagement whatsoever, amber meaning that there was some engagement and green highlighting that there was engagement. Using this, you could RAG rate (Red, Amber, Green) each session to see how well James engaged in each session and even how well he met the learning objective (see **Online Resources**).

Take this a step further: You can do this with all children up to the age of 11. Use forms of self-assessment to allow children to engage in assessing their own engagement and how well they meet the learning objective. Build on this by allowing children to make comments on the session, which can be taken back into class to support the teacher in becoming consistent in approaches to the behaviours presented.

Miss Lawrence thinks...	James thinks...
This week we have been discussing incidents where James has shouted out. He has been using the technique that we looked at last week of counting down from five when he feels like shouting out. He has been able to use this three times this week and has been successful. *Highlight your circles separately using your Red, Amber, Green system so that it is easy to see at a glance	I am really proud of myself this week. I was able to practise the counting down game when I felt like I was going to shout out. Miss Lawrence is happy with me. My friends are happy with me. My mum and dad are happy with me. I'm proud of myself this week.

Tapping/fidgeting

The following case study will discuss both tapping and fidgeting, the different ways in which they can present and a variety of strategies that will support you to eliminate them.

Case study: Kaylee – aged six

Kaylee is enthusiastic about learning and school. She is progressing well and is a high achiever. When she is sitting with the others for carpet time, she fidgets and finds it hard to stay in the same position. You spend a lot of time telling her to sit properly on the carpet. She taps others to get their attention during your input and, again, you spend a lot of time reminding her not to distract others. When she is at the table, she is constantly tapping her pencil and appears unable to keep it still. You're unsure how to approach it. It takes a lot of your time in dealing with it, but it's not affecting her work. She is still capable of achieving good-quality pieces of work.

Kaylee is a challenge for you. It's a daily struggle for you to decide whether to acknowledge this behaviour and deal with it or to ignore it and risk the possibility of it escalating. It's also a confusing struggle as, despite the amount of time that you are spending in dealing with her behaviour, she is still producing high-quality pieces of work.

Practical strategies to support Kaylee

1 – Visual reminders

One of the biggest problems identified would be that your flow of teaching is interrupted on a regular basis. Kaylee does need a reminder because, although it isn't affecting her own work, her behaviour is causing a detriment to others' learning. One way of helping Kaylee is through visual reminders.

Create yourself some visuals, identifying 'good listening', 'good looking' and 'good sitting' (see **Online Resources**). Discuss the use of these visuals during a PSHE lesson, without specific reference to Kaylee and her behaviour. The lesson could start off by discussing the key learning behaviours that are needed to have a successful lesson. Children could design their own 'good listening', 'good looking' and 'good sitting' posters. These posters are simple pictures that can go alongside these phrases, and which will act as a visual reminder to the child and will prompt them to show the positive behaviour you want to see.

Either use your own or some of the children's posters to have laminated and on display within your classroom. Then, during your teaching input, when Kaylee is fidgeting and/or tapping, simply point to the posters and continue with your input. This will have a direct impact, as you won't interrupt the flow of your lesson but it will bring attention to the expectations that you have of the children, including Kaylee, during your lesson.

Bear in mind that it may take some practice to be able to do this in a subtle manner, but it will pay off when you are able to support Kaylee with this at the same time as continuing the teaching. It will also minimise your own disruption.

> **Take this a step further:** You could direct your Learning Support Assistant (LSA) or, using discrete opportunities, praise Kaylee when she corrects her behaviour without having to be spoken to. Although you are drawing her attention to the visuals, she is still correcting her own behaviour. Kaylee will then begin to correct her own behaviour after continued opportunities to practise. Ensure that you keep praising her for this behaviour modification. Don't forget, praise can be simply a smile. It does not have to be an actual reward.

2 – Objects

Sometimes, children in Kaylee's position need something to fiddle with in order to concentrate. This does not need to be an expensive fiddle toy, although they can be fantastic to keep brains engaged. It can be something as simple as a piece of sticky tack.

Make sure that you have a conversation beforehand about why you have given them a fiddle toy and what the objective of this is. There must be rules around this. For example:

- Use your sticky tack/fiddle toy to help you to concentrate.
- It is YOUR sticky tack/fiddle toy and no one else's.

- You need to show 'good looking', 'good listening' and 'good sitting' at all times.

Review this as you would with an intervention to see its impact on the child's fidgeting and tapping. If it's successful, combine it with some activities around fidgeting so that the child can learn to control his/her own behaviour as well.

Take this a step further: *Through your ongoing work with your child, you can make your own fiddle toys. For example:*

- *Pipe cleaners – use pipe cleaners and twist them round each other.*

- *Bead strings – thread beads onto a simple shoelace. It will create a fantastic fiddle toy and it will be personal to the child.*

- *Nuts and bolts – the motion of turning the nuts around will act as a fiddle toy for the child so that they can concentrate during your input.*

Note – you must complete a risk assessment if using these fiddle toys, as they can be seen as a health and safety risk and must be used responsibly and only given with careful thought. Work with your head teacher and parents of the child when introducing a fiddle toy.

3 – Active/physical starter

We've already identified that Kaylee struggles during the input of a lesson. She struggles to sit still and avoid fidgeting. One method of supporting her would be to give her a physical or active starter. For example, if you are looking at Venn diagrams in your maths lesson, then put her into a small group who could be looking at this in an active way.

Grab two hoops, allow the children to decide the sorting criteria and organise objects according to this. The children will be accessing the learning objective. If you are using an LSA to support this group, then it can act as a 'pre-teach' for the lesson, which will add a basis for further progression. You may see an impact on Kaylee's concentration during that time, as well as an impact on her concentration during the lesson.

> *Take this a step further:* *Not all lessons will allow for an active starter. If you find that it does have a positive impact on her concentration, then there are other options available to you. Give Kaylee a jot book. She can write down her workings during your input. It is productive fidgeting! If a jot book is successful, implement a diary for English sessions and topic work. She can be making notes that will help to support her during table time as well as allow her to channel her thoughts and ideas in a more productive way.*

These low-level behaviours present in different ways, like those I will describe with Jayden. They will also need different approaches, using alternative strategies, so read through the two case studies before deciding how you will proceed.

Case study: Jayden – aged seven

Jayden is a happy, likeable and energetic boy who always appears over-excited, which can be exhibited in one of two ways: he can be energetic, work well and produce good outcomes or he can distract others, tap others, fidget and, on some occasions, hit others. He is always apologetic and his actions aren't targeted. He has friends within the class but the quieter members of the class shy away from Jayden, as he can be unpredictable.

Jayden responds differently to different members of staff. He does have the ability to develop relationships with adults but his mum reports that he can be misunderstood.

Similarly to James, it is important to consider the following:

Question: Has Jayden's low-level behaviour been present in previous years or has it just begun this year?

The SENDCo in your school may need to pursue other avenues in a situation similar to this, but it is also important for you to employ strategies to support Jayden and facilitate him in accessing learning within your classroom.

Practical strategies to support Jayden

1 – Relationships

The use of positive relationships will be vital to supporting Jayden. He already has good relationships with some members of staff. Direct these members of staff to act as mentors to Jayden when these behaviours are presented. It is important to build the relationships between Jayden and other members of staff so that we can provide him with a large support network.

One technique that is worth trying is timing slots. It only needs to be five opportunities a day of two-minute discussions. These discussions need to be led by Jayden and can be on a topic of his choice (it doesn't need to be education-focused).

This technique seems such a simple thing but we all know how easy it is to get lost in a school day, and setting aside time will enable you to begin that building of key relationships.

Take this a step further: *Embark on a joint project together. Build an F1 car or work on a comic together but, again, ensure this is child-led. During this time, you will build your relationship and will have a common interest and product at the end of it. You can use this later on in the year as a stimulus for conversation during a busy day.*

---

2 – Pick your battles

We alluded to the fact that Jayden can be rather unpredictable at times. Sometimes, you can channel his energy positively and there is no disruption to his learning and that of others. However, sometimes he can be over-excited and this can escalate. During these times, ensure that you are picking your battles wisely. You don't want to be picking up on absolutely everything that Jayden is doing but focusing on supporting him to be calm and refocus himself.

It is important that during this time you communicate well with your LSA, so they know that this is the technique that you are using and that they can use it too. This consistency will allow you to provide a structure for Jayden whilst you refocus his energy.

Take this a step further: Think of the Diamond 9 activity (page 9). Which behaviours come at the top? Focus on these and come back to the bottom-level behaviours at a later point.

3 – Brain breaks

If Jayden is really struggling and you cannot get him to refocus, then use your LSA to take him for a 'brain break'. It will allow him to release energy and endorphins and he will be able to refocus. Some examples of brain breaks are:

- Get a strong piece of elastic and allow Jayden to simply pull it as hard as he can. This pulling motion will allow him to exert energy.

- Allow Jayden to run as fast as he can around the field. Again, this will release additional energy for Jayden.

- Get Jayden to reach as high as he can and be as tall as he can be; this can be termed 'superhero stretching'. Jayden can be his favourite superhero during this time too! It will be a firm favourite with your children. It can also be used in a whole-class situation if you notice that other children need a brain break and not just Jayden.

The categories mentioned are not a finite list of low-level behaviours that you will experience in the classroom. The practical strategies are also not limited to the categories that they were put with. We know that strategies that work for some do not work for others and vice versa, so dip in and dip out of the different strategies. Use them, note them and review them.

There are a variety of practical strategies that you can employ to simply deal with and ultimately eradicate low-level behaviour:

1) Voice control – when the volume in your classroom becomes louder and louder, you may often, without thinking, raise your voice to try to compete. What happens when your voice reaches its maximum? You lose control. It is important that you are able to recognise when this is likely to happen and use your voice in a constructive way.

   When you use a quieter voice, you will find that your children respond positively to this and they will quieten to listen to you. Save your voice for dangerous situations. You will need children to take note when you use your 'loud voice', so save it for when you really need it.

2) Moods – children can enter your classroom without dealing with incidents in their minds from previous lessons, breaks or lunchtimes. Look at their body language. If they are not ready to come in, communicate with another adult and allow them a little talk break. If you don't have that luxury of additional help, then allow them responsibility – let them do a little job or take the register.

Also be mindful that adults can enter your classroom holding onto previous behaviour incidents. Allow them the time to debrief with somebody, and not necessarily you. You are in control in that classroom so don't allow a negative adult to enter. Be firm but honest. It will only impact in a negative way on your classroom.

3) Move around – use your physical presence in a positive way. If children are working in groups and you're noticing a child off-task, try not to confront them straight away. Head over with open body language and give them a fair verbal reminder – for example, 'You've made a great start. I'm heading over to look at Blue table now. I want to see two more sentences when I get back. I can't wait to see them!'. That positivity will spur children on to want to please you.

4) Be prepared – the truth is that if you are not prepared for your lesson, then low-level behaviour will bubble. Fully plan your lessons, have your resources out, brief your adults, declutter your classroom. If these foundations are firm, then there aren't easy opportunities for children to bubble. You can't get everything right but it is important to do everything that you can to avoid it.

5) Swap in – it is ok to find yourself getting annoyed with low-level disruption. Do not be afraid to swap in with someone else to give yourself time to calm down. It is that elephant in the room; those that do not recognise hot spots in themselves will find themselves annoyed, shouting and ultimately escalating the situation. Those that recognise this within themselves, swapping in and allowing themselves to calm down, will ultimately control the situation and minimise that disruption to learning and the classroom.

6) You – remember you are the decisive element in that classroom! If your mood is negative, the classroom will be negative. If you enter that classroom and feel confident in how the lesson will go, then it will be positive. Strategies that will support this include:

- Stand at the door as children and parents enter. Say hello to each and every child, regardless of behaviours exhibited on previous days. Every child deserves a blank slate on the following day. If you hold onto the previous day's behaviours, then you will simply encourage a repeat.

- Have conversations with children and parents. Encourage the relationship that will support you to unlock behaviours.

- Always say goodbye as they exit. It will end the day on a positive note for the children and allow you to provide that blank slate on the following day.

7) Positive language – the use of 'don't' with children has limited success. Use positive ways of correcting behaviour – for example, 'Don't rock on your chair!' turns into, 'We sit on our chairs nicely so that our handwriting is neat'.

We have gone through a lot of positive and practical strategies to support you with low-level behaviours. Don't try to implement them all at once, although hopefully you'll be buzzing with new ideas to try tomorrow! Take a couple, implement them and reap the rewards of the changes.

Chapter 3
Supporting children with passive behaviour

Passive behaviour would come under the umbrella of 'behaviour for learning'. The term 'behaviour for learning' has been bandied about a lot in primary schools, and for some time it had the potential to become a buzz word that people didn't really understand, let alone know how to implement. My interpretation of behaviour for learning is simply creating an environment that supports children to exhibit positive behaviour, allowing them to be 'learning ready'. An environment is not simply your classroom; it is your classroom, your vision, your atmosphere, **you!**

The key to positive behaviour for learning is relationships, and not just those between you and your child. The key relationships include the relationship that the child has with him/herself, the relationship that the child has with others and the relationship that the child has with his/her learning. As a teacher, it is your job to facilitate, build and empower these relationships.

Relationship that the child has with him/herself

This relationship can be the most fractious, difficult to repair and improve, as well as the source of many difficulties. It can also be the hardest to identify. A child that can appear to be extremely disruptive and sometimes over-confident can actually be the child with the lowest self-esteem. Facilitating self-esteem work and work around emotions can be extremely challenging. Imagine someone asking you to tell them your biggest secret or disclose your biggest weakness. How do you feel?

Vulnerable? Embarrassed? Like you want the ground to swallow you up? This is how your child feels if you suddenly start discussing self-esteem and feelings. It's where questioning is so important.

Schedule some time aside for you and your child to work together. You know that it is to build up self-esteem; they don't necessarily need to know. We will explore some practical strategies below that will enable you to help that child to build the relationship that he/she has with him/herself. Then we can have a look at some questions that you can weave into this time.

Idea 1 – Important to me

This is a simple and effective strategy, promoting an initial conversation with your child that actually gives you important information. Draw around your child's hand on a piece of paper. At the top of each finger and thumb, the child has to choose a person that is important to them. Don't limit this to a blood relation. Be mindful that sometimes our children are not living with their family and if you do limit it, then you could be having an adverse effect. This activity works even better if you do it alongside the child.

This can be used from early years right through to the end of primary school.

Idea 2 – I am amazing!

The hardest part of building a child's self-esteem is getting them to realise that they are amazing! This activity can be done in a variety of ways. You can either provide the child with an outline of a person or you can get outside and draw round the child in chalk. Then the child needs to label all the parts that are amazing about them. For example: 'I am amazing at football because I have converted five/six penalties', 'I am amazing because I have worked really hard on my handwriting and now I'm allowed to use a pen'. Again, it is important that you do it too. You may feel that sense of embarrassment, but you *are* amazing because there is that child that you want to invest in or else you wouldn't be reading this book!

This can be used from early years right through to the end of primary school.

Idea 3 – Opportunities

A simple, quick win for children is to provide them with opportunities to show off their strengths. By providing these opportunities over a longer period of time, it will become embedded in your classroom and have a positive impact on your children's self-esteem, allowing children to express themselves and, consequently, their strengths. A range of options can include supporting children to become members of the school council, creating sports ambassadors, using positive role models, etc.

Throughout all of these sessions, use questioning to build your relationship. Sometimes thinking of questions or how to lead a conversation can be difficult. To help you with finding the right questions, here are some key ideas to try. Read through these with the child that you want to work with in mind, and write down some key questions that you want to ask during your sessions.

- Ensure that your questions have a purpose – as much as you want to find out a lot of information, is it necessary?
- If there isn't an option to ask the question in your session, bank it for the next. Refrain from pushing it, despite your need.
- Always remember that you're there to build the child's self-esteem.

Relationships that the child has with others

This is an element that is so important for a child in order to access many parts of school life: friendships, working with a partner, team work, collaborating, and the list goes on. Consequently, it is important that we facilitate this carefully.

You can use a list like the one on page 30 to identify the area to focus on first. These activities can be used within intervention time to work on the difficulties that you have identified. Always start with one other positive role model unless specified.

> Does your child struggle with?
> Turn-taking
> Playing in a group
> Appropriate games
> Developing friendships
> Sustaining friendships
>
> Read on…

Idea 1 – Turn-taking

Taking turns, whether in a game or a conversation, is a skill that some children can find difficult. It may not have been a part of daily life for them and may not be a skill that has been taught or even expected of them. Therefore, you may need to provide an opportunity for your child to practise this – for example, with board games that you have already in your classroom. Start with you and your child, so that you can facilitate this process until your child is comfortable with taking turns, knowing when to take their turn and allowing others to have their go. Once you've reached that comfort level, where children are showing the ability to take turns, introduce a positive role model other than yourself for your child to play with. Continue the sessions, where you are providing these opportunities with you as a facilitator to help support the turn-taking. Build up until you can step away and your child can play confidently and take turns with another child.

Idea 2 – Playing in a group

Duck, duck, goose: A traditional game that introduces the idea of competition without it being overt. The game is played in a circle. Someone is chosen to walk around the outside of the circle, touching each child's head whilst calling 'duck' after each tap. The child then chooses someone, touches their head and says 'goose'. The 'goose' then has to jump up and chase the person who tags them, who will be running around the circle back into the 'goose's' place! If the 'goose' catches the tagger, then they win! If not, they lose and they are then the one to go around the circle, and so on.

To support those who struggle working in a group, I would start off by being with the child that finds working in a group difficult, so you can bring a sense of fun and light-heartedness to the game, particularly at those tricky moments.

Running alongside this, you can, at different points in the day, refer to the successes that your child has achieved during this game and even apply it to other times when they need to use teamwork. For example, 'I know that you can work with Jane on this project. Do you remember when we played 'Duck, duck, goose'? You showed me such fantastic teamwork. Let's apply it to this.'

Parachute games: Have a look through your PE cupboard and see if you can find a parachute. Normally used for team-building games, it will be perfect to build collaborative skills within your child. If you don't have one, then you can always use a sheet instead. It's really important that you start this off with only one other child, as the child you are focusing on will be having difficulty not only with working in a group but also with the skill of being able to use the parachute! Try the following activities with your small group:

- Wave the parachute up and down at the same time as each other. It sounds easy but have a go! It takes practice!

- Throw a sponge ball into the equation. Try to roll it around the edge of the parachute without it falling off.

- Bounce the ball on the parachute ten times without it falling off!

- Roll the ball to each other along the parachute.

These tasks aren't easy and require concentration and resilience. Again, you are able to refer to this when things are getting difficult in a school task; you can say: 'I know that you can do this maths question. It may seem tricky now but remember how hard we found the parachute task and look at how good we were at that by the end!'.

Idea 3 – Fun games to play with your child

We cannot and should not have control over what parents class as appropriate games for their children, but it does influence the behaviour and games that enter our playgrounds. It's also a topic that can be controversial with teachers, in terms of what is appropriate and what is not. There may be a member of staff who insists that no child is allowed to play with an imaginary gun, or another insisting that children play with a ball of a certain material or of a certain size above any other, which is why it is important to speak to all staff and discuss what is deemed appropriate at your school individually.

Early Years

With a child under five, the curriculum should be designed around play. There are plenty of opportunities for imaginary play within the curriculum. For a child struggling to understand what play appropriate for their age actually is, it is important to support the child during this time, so that they can understand what they should and shouldn't be playing. Select materials such as cardboard and show the child how to play with it – how it can be made into a rocket, for example. The better they get at imaginary play, the easier it will be to begin removing the adult support, and the child will be able to play alongside others appropriately.

Five to seven years

Even at these ages, children may not understand how to play appropriately with other children, and you may need to support them in the activities. Plan one of your group sessions as follows:
 Choose your group wisely. Have your targeted child in a group with no more than three positive role models.

- Explain your objective: to be able to play a game together.
- Start your discussion with a mind map: 'What games would most children aged six to seven like?'. Throughout this discussion, you can tease out answers that are age-appropriate with the children.
- Once you have an age-appropriate list, you can select a game, discuss the rules and then play with the group. It means that not only can you demonstrate appropriate games to the children but you can also support them with their social skills.

This can be also adapted to use in your SEMH interventions and reviewed after six weeks to measure impact. Interventions can be implemented in your school day in order to build up children's social skills or support them with their emotional development and/or mental health.

Seven to eleven years

There isn't much of a difference in approach between children aged four and 11 years old, but you can add more discussion as children get older. You can talk about the appropriateness of the certificate in computer games and the themes that come through. You can also discuss the behaviour of famous sports people and why some behaviours shouldn't transfer onto your school football field – for example, swearing on the pitch and diving to gain a penalty.

> **Top Tip:** When introducing appropriate games, there may be a child who appears disengaged and unenthusiastic, perhaps because they are desensitised to age-appropriate games. This is where it is vital for you to be aware of yourself as support. Be as enthusiastic as you can when introducing these games. Show genuine joy and the children will rediscover their joy.

Case study: Luke – aged four

Luke was a child who played a variety of computer games that weren't appropriate for his age. He often talked in detail about playing *Call of Duty* and *Grand Theft Auto* at home. He tried to engage others within the playground to pretend to steal cars and shoot prostitutes. When children didn't want to play, he could become aggressive and refuse to play their games. He referred to them as 'babyish'. I knew that I'd have to overcome defensive behaviours when I first started to support Luke with play.

I first introduced some simple playground games with him. I assumed he had an interest in cars, judging by the computer games that he had played, so I took out a car mat and some toy cars. I led the play. Luke came in and out of the game, classing it as 'boring'; however, when he wasn't engaged, he was watching from afar. Over time, he engaged and enjoyed playing. From this, I played other playground games, including throwing beanbags into targets and skipping games. Luke was able to engage in these and went on to be able to do this independently.

Idea 4 – Developing friendships

Friendship is such an important issue during school. Whether your children feel like it is important to them or not – it is! It is also vital to their learning, regardless of their ability, whether it be discussing an idea with a partner, justifying their opinions or developing mastery by explaining their thoughts.

Early Years

'My name is... and I like...': This activity is exactly as it sounds. You can sit in a circle with the group that you are trying to support in friendship. Start by modelling your name and an activity that you like. For example: 'My name is Tracey and I like playing with diggers'. You then go around the circle and each child contributes. You can facilitate the development of friendships by highlighting the commonalities: 'WOW! Jack, I didn't realise that you liked diggers too!'. Not only are you modelling friendship starter conversations, but you are also opening up similarities for free play, when Jack may invite someone over to play with his diggers.

Five to eight years

Fun art: You may have taught the drawing of self-portraits before by using a mirror, but this activity involves another child. Partner your child up with someone that you want to support a friendship with. Explain that their activity is to draw a portrait of their partner. Meanwhile, have some questions on your IWB (interactive whiteboard) that the children need to find out about their partner. They could be anything that can start conversation, but some examples could be:

- What is your favourite colour?
- Who is your favourite singer?
- What is your favourite programme on TV?
- What is your best/worst food?

Key Stage 2

Friendship bingo: You can play this game in a whole-class setting or in a group. Give each child a grid with different statements, such as

'... likes chips', '... plays Minecraft', '... loves football' or '... speaks French'. Explain that the objective of the game is to find someone that can match each of the grid statements. You can introduce the rule that they must find someone different for each square, but that depends on your group. You don't want to make this a hard activity for someone who already finds it difficult to make new friends.

Idea 5 – Sustaining friendships

Developing friendships is one thing but sustaining those friendships is a whole other difficulty. Children struggle to sustain friendships within school, and as a teacher you are constantly supporting children with their friendships. The amount of conflict resolution that you have to do after an hour's lunchbreak can be a test for any primary teacher!

Conflict resolution can sound complicated but it is a simple strategy that can facilitate any friendship. You have to be clear about the process. If there's a disagreement between friends, then it is important that you stop the children trying to compete to have their story heard first. Signal 'STOP' by holding your hand in the air so that you can start the process. Invite one child to speak first but insist that, during this time, the other does not interrupt at all, and reassure them that they will get their time to talk. Once they have finished their version of events then invite the other child to speak. Your role is not to judge, just to listen and facilitate. Once both have discussed the incident, ask the question, 'How can we move forward?'. Once you've agreed your ways forward, allow the children to act upon it. The more that the children have a chance to practise their conflict resolution, the better that they will become at completing the process. They may be able to do this for themselves in the future!

Relationship that the child has with learning

Stand at the back of your class when you are delivering the next input during a lesson and look for learning. Look for the reaction of your children – are they engaged? Are they actively participating with your input?

If not, then you can tinker with aspects of your lessons to check that it isn't the curriculum that the children are disengaged with:

- Are your lessons designed to support children's learning? Are they targeted correctly – to support? To challenge and extend? If they aren't targeted properly, then children may become demotivated early on.

- Are your lessons designed for brain breaks? Are children subject to high-paced lessons, where they need to have brain breaks to take the opportunity to reset, recharge and reinvigorate, ready to fire again into lessons?

- Are your lessons exciting? Now, don't take this personally! Remember that we are on a journey, and part of our behaviour journey is being honest with ourselves, so look at your plan. Will your children be excited by it? There is a lot of criticism over the use of learning styles but it's still important to ensure that your lessons *are* physical, visual, etc. They need to appeal to your children and excite them with their learning.

If you can honestly answer these questions with 'yes' then we need to look at reinvigorating behaviour for learning at a whole-school level.

Character

In December 2014, the Department for Education announced the desire to instil character in pupils. Nicky Morgan (education secretary at the time) wanted schools to provide opportunities for all young people to develop the character that they need to succeed in modern Britain. They had identified that our children tended to lack the resilience and character traits to allow them to be successful. They also identified that children needed to be well-rounded when they left school. Your school may support character development well but making it explicit to the success of learning is a whole-school vision, where you need buy-in from all members of staff.

Where do you start?

1. Identify character traits that you decide are key ingredients for successful learners, such as resilience, self-efficacy, independence and collaboration.

2. Decide how you will tie them into your daily life – slow and thoughtful changes tend to be more sustainable.

Top Tip: *This will be even better if you can gain support, ideas and vision from your key stakeholders. At each point, engage with your school council. What do they see as key ingredients? Are there commonalities between your vision and the visions of your colleagues and governors? Better collaboration during these early stages will result in a higher chance of that sustainable change being embedded.*

Practical ideas to build resilience into daily life

Idea 1 – Sport

Sport is one of the simplest ways to support character development. Educate your teachers in the character traits that you have chosen as key ingredients. Explain that you expect your teachers to embed this vocabulary during sports sessions. Children will see each character trait needed to be successful in sport. They will learn resilience after a loss and, facilitated by a teacher, will learn collaboration, leading to success in the future.

Idea 2 – Learn about vocabulary

Ask each year group to choose one of the character words. Teach your class about that word throughout a week. What does it mean? What effect would it have on you, on others in your class or on the school? Ask them to think about how this would present within a person. Allow your children to present their ideas in any way that they want, whether it be through art work, movie-making or word clouds. At the end of a week, get the whole school together in assembly and present your word as a class. At the end of this assembly, the whole school will have knowledge of at least six different character words. Use these as your foundation. You can repeat this activity again at another point to take on another set of words.

Idea 3 – Display

Think about how you will change the learning environment to reflect your new character curriculum. You could gather a group of children and get them to mind map artistic ideas for each character word. They could paint this onto an individual canvas so that you end up with a piece of artwork for each word. These can be displayed all around your school to support your new atmosphere and bring a sense of community and empowerment to your learning environment.

Idea 4 – School awards

Most schools have some form of awards within school to celebrate academic successes. Some even go further and look at behaviour, friendship, etc. Small amendments could be made for these to reflect, develop and celebrate character traits. Instead of having 'Sports Person of the Week', you could look at the traits needed to be successful in this and rename it 'Collaboration Award'. When giving the award, you can also explain why that person was successful.

> **Top Tip:** Go one step further and ask children to nominate each other for the character traits that they spot in each other.

Idea 5 – Integrate character traits into your lessons

Keep the character vocabulary in your mind and refer to it during your lessons. For example, in an art lesson, explain to the children that they will need creativity for the lesson. You could even refer to previous success if children question their ability. For example: 'You can do this really easily. Remember when you used your creativity for that other project. You can definitely do this now!'. Make sure that your children know that the only person in control of their character is them.

> **Top Tip:** Include character vocabulary in your learning objectives and success criteria.

Teachers are always keen to try new ideas. They see an idea, they take it and they use it. It's a great way of ensuring that the best practice is in our classroom, impacting on the progress and learning of our children. It's the reason that you're reading this book – to see, take and use. This next idea is one that I used in my setting.

Idea 6 – Behaviour for Learning Driving Licence

The Behaviour for Learning Driving Licence was created with all credit to Mark Oldman and his team at Millgate School in Leicester. He presented at a Behaviour TeachMeet (more on this in Chapter 10). The Driving Licence is an idea that was implemented at whole-school level, so you will need to have had open discussions with staff and SLT to see whether it is useful in your setting. I always recommend that you change it for your setting, as I did for mine.

The idea is that children 'graduate' through the different stages, in order to qualify for their 'driving licence'. These stages are:

- initiate (first gear)
- interact (second gear)
- involve (third gear)
- imagine (fourth gear)
- innovate (fifth gear)
- inspire (top gear).

In order for the children to progress through the different gears, they need evidence to show that they have met the different requirements, which is why you need that whole-staff buy-in. Evidence can be identified in every part of school life, so your communication with teachers, midday staff, support staff and volunteers is crucial. Children aren't expected to get through the different gears in a year; this is a journey. Again, you can discuss this with other members of staff to see what is appropriate for you.

To go through the different gears, school staff have to see that children are showing evidence of consistently meeting the requirements in each gear. The different requirements are as follows:

Initiate (first gear)

Have you regularly…

- removed your coat when coming into a lesson?
- sat down quietly?
- written the date on your work?
- listened to instructions?

- followed instructions?
- completed tasks that have been asked of you?
- presented work neatly?

This 'gear' is designed to allow children to experience quick success. The majority of your children will be able to complete these requirements with ease and/or without too much demand on themselves. The children that will struggle to complete these requirements will be those that you will be looking at providing interventions for. We are talking about the majority of children in this chapter, and providing as much support as you can to engage them in their learning.

Interact (second gear)

Do you continually...

- participate in class discussions and activities?
- listen to the ideas of others?
- ask for support when needed?
- engage throughout the lesson?
- trust your teacher when they are extending you and pushing you in your work? Embrace the challenge!

This is designed to push your children a little bit more. Some children may need support in this area, as it relies on the children being able to have good relationships with others – an idea expanded on earlier in this chapter. If you foresee a child struggling in this area, spread out their successes in the requirements so that children can experience success weekly or bi-weekly. Meanwhile, you can be putting in some supportive work, as detailed in Chapter 2, so that the transition through this gear seems smoother for the children.

Involve (third gear)

Are you often willing to...

- listen and respond to the ideas of others?
- take responsible risks?
- make mistakes when pushing yourself? Do you have a resilient attitude to this?

- revisit your work and improve?
- encourage other children to join in with you?
- ask sensible questions?

Mistakes can be one of the biggest barriers that you can have as a child. Some children can fly through primary school without hitting that time where they make a mistake or meet failure. It is *our* job to prepare our children not only for secondary school but also for adult life. I'm not suggesting that we deliberately set our children up for failure but, by building a culture where children can make a mistake without judgement, you are also supporting those children that may respond badly when they do hit that wall. Make mistakes yourself when completing a task, whether it is making a spelling mistake or making an error in maths; model the attitude and facilitate children's responses. In this way, you are building your children up to have a programmed response for when it does happen. And, as my colleague always says, 'Mistakes make your brain grow!'

Imagine (fourth gear)

Can you…

- work independently?
- think creatively?
- relate your lesson to previous learning?
- ask probing questions?

There's a sense of maturity to this gear. Children have to do so much in school before they are able to work independently. How can you help support children to work independently before they are able to do it? A 'help' board is a great way of supporting through display. In my classroom, I have a series of steps embedded before children need to ask an adult. Often a child's first response is to put their hand up and seek an adult – learned helplessness. As the class teacher, you can scaffold children to become more independent. On your help board, start off by having a section for 'stop and think!'. Encourage your children to take the time to think for themselves for ways of solving the problem that is stopping them from completing their work. The next section could be to speak to their partner to see whether they can support them. I would always suggest teaching your children explicitly that helping someone is not the same as telling somebody the answers! You can complete PSHE work around supporting others so that children are clear on the expectations of supporting others.

Innovate (fifth gear)

Could you...

- direct your own learning?
- think flexibly and approach learning in more than one way?
- persist and change your approach until you succeed?
- reflect on your progress over time?

Reflection is vital for growing as a learner. Encourage children to reflect through self-assessment right through from four to 11 years old. The next step would be to move to peer assessment. Again, this is a skill that needs teaching or you'll end up with comments for comments' sake – for example, 'Little Jimmy is amazing at everything. Doesn't need to do anything to improve!'. Building that culture of support will help us to be honest with each other in learning. Taking that reflection a step further and supporting a child to reflect on their own progress in learning, rather than simply on one piece of work, can be easier than you think! Once the above is embedded, begin to provide children with an opportunity to reflect every term. This can be a simple self-report, looking at different areas of learning. Take English, for example. What have children learnt during that term? You can remind them of what you have covered. Get them to discuss with a partner what their next steps would be to improve further. Complete this with all areas of learning. You may get simple responses to begin with but, as you practise this skill of reflection more, they will ask more of themselves.

Once you have your adapted idea to promote positive behaviour for learning, the most important thing is to sell it to your children! Excite them and enthuse them about the idea. You need to show them how important it is to 'start their journey'. Mark did it through a YouTube video created by his staff; I would use a Prezi (online presentation tool). However you do it, ensure that it creates that buzz!

Inspire (top gear)

Might you...

- teach others?
- inspire others to learn?
- create opportunities for peers to develop and succeed?

One of the best parts of the job is to watch children teaching each other.

Case study: Toby – aged ten

Toby is a looked after child (LAC), a term which applies when a child has been taken into care, either temporarily or on a permanent basis. He has been in a variety of foster care placements but is now settled in his long-term placement. Toby shows great leadership qualities, gets involves with any opportunities that he can and joins every single sporting team.

Louis, who is six, has just been removed from the care of his mother. He is in a long-term foster home with a foster family whom he absolutely adores! However, the impact of this change was felt at school. Behaviour was heightened and it was difficult to keep him in mainstream school. Through support from external agencies, we were able to support Louis with his behaviour and reduce his anxieties. Louis is a happy boy and enjoys school now. He is keen to show his affection and is always smiling. His foster carer has just taken on a short-term placement for two other boys.

Toby approached me to say that this can be a particularly difficult time for a foster child and offered his support for Louis. I agreed and Toby came over to work with Louis.

Toby prepared his own materials for his session with Louis. They laughed, they chatted, they drew and they bonded.

During this time, Toby taught Louis. It wasn't academic; he taught him vital and invaluable skills that he needed during this time. Toby is without a doubt in that top gear.

I'm sure that you have ideas already about what you want to implement to support behaviour for learning within your school. Grab a notepad, scribble down your ideas and prioritise them. It takes time to change a culture so don't be disappointed if you're trying to use the whole-school ideas and aren't seeing change immediately!

Chapter 4
Extreme behaviours

Although titled 'extreme' behaviours, our definitions of extreme can be very different; however, the feelings that it conjures up are exactly the same – that panic that you feel when you think that you have run out of strategies to support and modify behaviour, that very panic that makes you question whether you can *actually* do this.

The first step is to think about the situation in a practical way, which is what this chapter aims to do. There are methods of thinking about behaviour practically, some of which are detailed below.

Behaviour as a form of communication

You may have heard of this as a motto or inspirational quote but it is true. With behaviour, whether the child is shouting, pushing or throwing things, there is an underlying effort at communication. It could be frustration, the fact that they have had a disagreement on the playground or something that is happening within their lives but, regardless, they cannot find the words to explain themselves or their feelings. It may even be that they do not have the language to express themselves. Furthermore, they might not even know what it is that they are trying to communicate. But they are, and to understand the reasons behind the more extreme behaviours, you need to learn how to help translate this form of communication.

A key strategy in translating this communication is understanding the cause. An ABC chart, a simple table where you can note down individual behavioural incidents, can support you in this. 'Antecedent' looks at where the incident took place and anything that may have led to it. 'Behaviour' determines the actual behaviour presented, whether it be physical aggression or verbal. 'Consequence' details what happened as a result. Sometimes, when using the ABC chart (see **Online Resources**), you look for frequency in incidents, but it can also be extremely useful in spotting possible causes for the behaviours that were presented during this incident. If the frequency in behaviours is high first thing in the morning, then it may be useful to introduce a 'meet and greet'.

Meet and Greet

Children can appear up and down in the morning and their emotions can vary from being withdrawn to being excitable. A meet and greet can support a child by helping them to calm down in preparation for beginning the day in a smoother way.

Choose the person that is going to do the meet and greet carefully. It needs to be somebody that has a calm manner and can be engaging. It is their job to engage in conversation with the child first thing. They can do this through a variety of different ways:

- discussing any hobbies that they may have engaged in
- open questions for children who may appear withdrawn in order to encourage extended discussion
- calmly discussing the activities that will be happening today to prepare the child for the day ahead
- checking whether they've had any breakfast
- asking them to join you on some jobs that you could do.

Be conscious of how extreme behaviours may make you feel. Don't be afraid to swap in with a colleague if your 'buttons' are being pressed for the sake of keeping a situation as calm as you can. You may be feeling quite negative about the situation that you are in. It is quite easy for me to remind you to keep positive in the situation but it is vital to separate the child from the behaviours that are presented. A practical strategy to support you in this is the '5 x 2 strategy'.

5 x 2 strategy

When a child is presenting with regular difficult behaviour, you may find that your interactions with them can be continually negative unless you make a conscious effort to focus on also including positive conversations. The 5 x 2 strategy is a simple one. Make the effort to have a short two-minute conversation with your child at least five times a day. Just engage them in discussion and let them lead. It will ensure that there are positive points to their day and to yours.

Behaviour as a result of SEND

When extreme behaviour is presented, it can be a result of SEND. There can be two directions with this. A child's SEND may have already been diagnosed. In this case, the first thing that you need to do is to have a detailed conversation with the previous class teacher, the SENDCo and the child's parents. Depending on the level of SEND, there may be the following information available to you:

- An Individual Education Plan (IEP) – there is no legal requirement to keep an IEP for a pupil but, in the majority of cases, there are targets that are worked towards and places for other information, including strategies on how to support a child's individual needs.

- SEND support plan – if a child's needs are complex and require support additional to that of quality first teaching, then your SENDCo will have applied for this. Quality first teaching is you – your teaching. Some children require more input than this, such as regular intervention groups or one-to-one. As a school, you are required to fund the first £6,000 of support for a child. When the costs exceed this – for example, by requiring one-to-one support – then this is the route needed to ensure that your child is able to have the opportunities to make progress to the best of their ability. Through this, you may have access to a variety of reports, such as educational psychologist reports and social and health reports. Please don't be worried by the amount of jargon in them. Sit down with your SENDCo, who will be used to these terms. Ask for the key points, advice and recommendations. There are absolute jewels for support hidden amongst those scary terms! As part of this, there may be a one-page profile, which is a fantastic document explaining all about your children from their and their parents' perspectives. It helps you to fulfil that golden rule of developing relationships with the children themselves.

- Education, Health and Care Plan (EHCP) – if a child requires a move to alternative provision, such as a specialist school, then they will have an EHCP. It is a more detailed plan, with short- and longer-term aids. Within it you will find the key information that will help you in supporting your child to achieve their potential, managing their anxieties and understanding their diagnosis.

Use the expertise already gained as part of the process conducted to get an EHCP. There will be specialised reports to read that will provide you with detailed and individual strategies. Parents know their child and will have supported similar strategies. They may have lists of strategies that work and may even have advice on what to avoid. Depending on age and ability, your child may be able to be involved in these conversations as well. The value of this is high; pupil voice is integral in success. If it's possible for you, then do it!

The other direction may be when a child has SEND that is undiagnosed. To ensure that we are working towards positive outcomes for your child, then it is important to be engaging with the SENDCo, who will be able to investigate different routes in the SEND diagnosis programme. Meanwhile, the advice would remain the same. Use your key experts – parents, children, previous teachers and SENDCos – in order to find the most successful strategies.

Sometimes it can be a little intimidating or unnerving to seek support from parents. Trying to find support for difficult behaviour can evoke feelings of worry and stigma, but don't let this hinder you and impact on your ultimate aims of supporting your child. You may have really proactive parents, who are able to communicate clearly and engage with you over their child. However, you can also come across parents who aren't so engaged, not through any fault of their own – they may have had negative experiences with school in the past, including the one where you are teaching, or they may have been undervalued. It is key to build up this relationship.

You may have already used the 'Tips on having conversations with parents about behaviour' in Chapter 2, but engaging with them goes that level deeper. Here are some ideas for engaging parents without putting pressure where it isn't necessary.

Idea 1 – Value their input

We know that in school you can feel like you're running at 100 miles per hour – you possibly are! But it is important to think about how you are perceived and whether you're coming across as being disengaged, which you may well be when you have a to-do list as long as your arm and meetings set up that you know will involve confrontation. Whenever you are having meetings or informal contact with parents, breathe and let everything else go. Smile. Converse. It will put parents at ease and they will be more likely to engage with you, as you will be more engaging yourself.

Ask for their input at all different stages. Ask them what targets they feel are the next step for their child. Ask them whether they think that they have met their target. Listen when they show you evidence of successful strategies or evidence for learning. Together, you will be much stronger and be more likely to support the child for the better.

Idea 2 – Fun times

Share the positive moments, whether that's sharing a great piece of work or making a positive comment about the child's day. Personally invite the parent(s) in to attend any enrichment activities that you are holding, so that they know that you value the relationship. Allow them to see their child enjoying their school days. Sometimes parents can get swallowed up with the amount of targets that they see and reports that they read. Remind them that their child *is* enjoying their education and that you value the good times. It's good to reference these in later conversations as well.

Idea 3 – Parents as experts

As you find out more about your parents and deepen that relationship, you will begin to know their strength - use these. If one of their parents works in a bank, invite them in to support the money work that you will be doing in maths. You will find a whole host of professions within your classroom – artists, musical talent, even footballers. The experience that this will provide for your children will be amazing. You never know – you may even find some classroom volunteers!

All of these pointers and ideas will help you to engage your parents and build the sense of a team. Each of you will find yourself more at ease. Don't just forget this at the end of this year. Build on it and involve the next teacher, aiming for clear and secure communication for the child's whole school life.

Regardless of whether the behaviour is a result of SEND, communication issues and/or other reasons, you will need effective parental involvement for consistency when it comes to an IBP, which I'll take you through now.

Individual behaviour plans (IBPs)

This is going to be one of your main tools for consistency within school. It may also be one of the first effective strategies that you are able to implement when dealing with extreme behaviours. It can secure outcomes and quicken progress when communicated to everyone, and everyone is on board, but it is useless if used incorrectly.

Question: When should I have a behaviour plan in place?

If a child is presenting with behaviours that require much more focus than the other children in your class, then an individual behaviour plan may be suitable. If a child is presenting with behaviours that can be deemed a risk to themselves or others, then you will definitely need a plan.

Your SENDCo or behaviour manager may have a process in place for identifying whether a child needs to be placed on a plan. They may also have a 'cause for concern'. Some schools have this as a starting point. It details the areas that concern you as a teacher. This may be learning in English, it may be specifically behaviour at unstructured times. The most important way of identifying how to best support a child is note-taking. It may start simply as a diary of incidents that have happened, so that you can eradicate any kind of targeted behaviour, but the most effective tool for beginning to identify any patterns is the ABC chart.

ABC chart: A = Antecedent, B = Behaviour, C = Consequence (see **Online Resources**)

You can use this in so many different ways:

- Spotting hot spots – do behaviours occur more during a certain subject or in a certain place in school - for example, a cloakroom? Are there more incidents on a particular day of the week? By looking at this you are able to understand and prepare more. Can you move pegs in the cloakroom to the end so that you can minimise opportunities for misbehaviour? Can you introduce a meet and greet on a Monday to settle the child more? Can you provide the child with strategies to cope with a particular subject or introduce a now/next board? This is a visual way of showing your child what they are doing now and what will be coming after, and can be pictorial or written (see **Online Resources**).

- Support intervention – look at the behaviours presented. Organise them in terms of frequency, using the Diamond 9 resources mentioned in Chapter 2 (page 9), and use this to target intervention sessions. Organise your block of interventions focused on these and link them into your behaviour plans. When you are seeing positive moves forward, then redo your Diamond 9 to be able to target your next series of interventions.

- Identify what works – look at the consequences that you have implemented. Have any of them had an impact on a child's behaviour? Over a short period of time or long term? Are parents finding the same? Are other teachers finding the same?

Top Tip: *This could quite easily turn into you listing every single thing the child has done that is considered to be wrong, or it may even become a 'threat' ('stop that or else I'll write it down on the chart'), but it is your job to make sure that it isn't used in these ways. You could be the only person to note incidents in the ABC chart, or simply ensure that is treated in a relaxed way.*

Question: What should be in an IBP?

The most important aspect of an IBP is what's in it, as communicating it effectively is key. There is no requirement of how it should look, but it needs to be useful for you and your colleagues. It needs to be reviewed as often as behaviours change and should be a document that has been compiled by you and your colleagues. It needs to be shared with all members of staff that work with the child, so that consistency can be achieved, and needs to be on hand as a working document. Here are some helpful pointers of what to include:

- A picture of the child – speak to a member of staff who works in your school office. Usually there is an up-to-date photograph on file that you may be able to use or you can find one that you may have taken as part of school work. Remember that this is a working document that needs to be able to be picked up in a time of crisis. If a member of staff is involved that doesn't necessarily work with your child much, then they need to be aware of which child the plan applies to.

- Triggers – these are unique to your child and can be specific events, subjects, foods or smells that may usually trigger them to display difficult behaviours. You can't necessarily avoid these but being mindful of them will help to support your child.

- Escalating behaviours – have these split into primary and secondary behaviours? What behaviours are you seeing from the child? Secondary behaviours will be those behaviours that show you as a teacher that you may be heading towards a crisis. These are bound to be different for each child, depending on how severe their behaviour is, but I'd describe these as 'bubbly' behaviours – for example, tapping pencils or calling out. Primary behaviours are those behaviours that show you that a child is in crisis and needs your help to de-escalate. These could be such things as hurting others, hurting themselves or throwing furniture.

- Strategies – what strategies work for supporting your child to cease their difficult behaviours? These need to have some sort of hierarchy, so that one strategy can be undertaken before the next. They may involve swapping in different members of staff to support the child – for example, adjacent year group partners, year/age group coordinators, members of the senior leadership team, etc.

- Calming down – once your child has reached their crisis point, they will need your support in calming themselves down. Once calm, there needs to be a restorative conversation, where you are able to talk about an incident, discuss how to mend the situation and talk about what could have happened instead. The calming-down process may not be easy. You need to be specific about what strategies to use. Some children may respond to some thinking time – for example, 'I will give you five minutes alone and then I'll come and see whether you are ready to talk'. The time that you are providing for your child will give them that chance to think about their options in a quiet space and give them that very important opportunity to calm down. Time is your friend here. Think about yourself when you have really felt angry – you need time for the adrenaline to settle. Go back; if they're not ready, then repeat your script and give them another five minutes. When they are ready, take a walk to a different room and get them a drink of water. Finally, when they are calm, discuss the incident. You may discuss the impact of others or strategies that they tried to use to calm them and/or choices that they had, but the important thing is to get them talking.

- Positives – it also needs to be clear what will happen when the child chooses the right behaviours. When children are showing positive choices – such as following instructions or walking away from situations – then they could be rewarded, with a phone call or a positive text home, for example.

- History – this can be a short box that simply has an update of what has been submitted, such as SALT (Speech and Language Therapy) form submitted or educational psychologist report received.

- Other – this includes siblings in school and other factors on a need-to-know basis, such as the fact that they live with grandparents.

Question: How often should I update their IBP?

It is important to be having regular conversations with all staff involved with the child, their behaviours and their progress. It's during this time that you should go through the behaviour plan, even if it is just a brief scan, and look to see whether the different parts are still relevant. Have the behaviours changed? Have you noticed any more hot spots, methods for de-escalation or ways of calming down?

If you are making changes, view it as you do an IEP. It is a working document. Scribble on it, amend it but don't forget to share the changes.

Methods of dealing with extreme behaviour

By thinking of how you deal with behaviour and your strategies, you will be able to support more effectively. It's important to keep calm and level-headed during these times. Build your support networks, both in and out of school, so that you can 'switch off' as well as think strategically.

Extreme behaviours can bring about a whole host of different situations that you may have never seen before, such as behaviours that you have not previously been exposed to and physical restraint. These can cloud your judgements, as they aren't easy to deal with. However, in your job as a class teacher, you have that duty of care to support all of your children as well as provide equal access to education for all. Try to think of behaviour in the same way as you think of academia. If there is a gap in knowledge, you support children to achieve. If there is a gap in behaviour, you support children to progress.

Non-violent communication is a communication process that was developed by Marshall Rosenburg in the 1960s. It looked at three different aspects of communication: self-empathy, empathy and honest self-expression. Self-empathy is a deep, compassionate awareness of your own inner experience; empathy is understanding and sharing an emotion with others; and honest self-expression is expressing yourself genuinely in a way that will inspire compassion within others. It's based on the theory that all humans have the capacity for compassion and only resort to difficult behaviour when they cannot recognise more effective strategies for meeting their needs. This links into the thought that behaviour is communication and we need to unlock the strategies to help children to communicate more effectively.

There are ways of supporting yourself, and a range of methods that you may want to choose.

Alternative provision

There may be schools around your local area that help to provide support for your children, be it effective interventions, advice for support staff or support in deciphering targets. Don't view alternative provision as a separate entity. Collaboration is powerful, so use their advice as proactively as you can. Have a conversation, seek their advice and listen to their experiences.

Some PRUs and special schools have free outreach services and can come and support you in your setting. Call your local specialist provision to see how to access this support. For some it is a telephone referral, and for others there may be a referral form. Other provisions offer advice via a panel, where a group of colleagues come together to share experiences and previously used strategies, which can help with clarity and progress with your child. Again, call your local provisions to discuss ways that you can refer.

Restorative approaches

Restorative practice centres around creating a sense of belonging for our children – increasing a child's ability to develop social relationships with others, as well as restore these relationships when they go wrong. With children displaying these more extreme behaviours, our intervention is required even more. We need to be aware of relationships that are forming and support children during this time.

As a teacher, you need to know the benefits of an approach and the ways to implement it. As there are reams of evidence and information about this available, here is just a brief introduction.

The main benefits that you will see if you implement this approach are based around relationships. You know that your relationships can support or have a negative impact on a situation so, in improving this area, you can also improve the harmony within your classroom. You will head towards a relationship rather than implementing sanctions as a way of managing behaviours. You will work towards a community where children take responsibility and are more honest about their actions. Most of all, you will have built an environment where there are better relationships amongst staff and other children.

When there has been a behaviour incident within your classroom and you embark on restorative practice, you may need to focus on some of the following through your facilitation:

- effective communication within your class
- friendships and other relationships
- respect, empathy, repairing damage and even understanding the impact of your children's behaviour on others in the class.

Although these elements are your focus for restoration, you may find that there is a sense of restoration within the individual, whether it be secure boundaries for the child, self-confidence or self-respect.

Practical steps to take

You are the facilitator, so you need to cultivate responses to the following questions:

- What has happened?
- What has been the impact on those involved in the incident?
- What needs to happen to make things right?
- How can this be avoided next time?

As a teacher, I'm sure these questions are familiar to you, but you do need to ensure that you are building a culture of restorative practice consistently. There will be times where you will not be facilitator but you do need to ensure that other members of staff that will take on this have the following qualities:

- have a good rapport with pupils
- have a calming influence over what could be a heated exchange
- able to sit back, not jump in/interrupt and be an active listener
- trustworthy
- able to encourage your children to express themselves honestly

- able to appreciate the impact of a child's thoughts, feelings, beliefs and unmet needs on their behavioural choices.

If you want to implement this in your classroom, there are a couple of practical ideas to do this consistently.

Idea 1 – Lanyard card

Have the key questions on a card. If you have a school ID lanyard then these could fit on the back. If not, it should be something that can easily be carried around. This is another way of supporting your classroom staff. You or others may be coming into this restoration from somewhere else, and a little refresher on the key questions may be helpful.

Idea 2 – Model

Your colleagues need to be clear on the process and knowledgeable about the principles. If you've had whole-school training, then continue this by modelling these restorative conversations. It's good practice to coach using this model so you've all had experience in observing others delivering the conversation. It keeps things fresh and allows opportunities for questions and discussions around difficult conversations.

Case study: Amy – aged five

Amy is new to the school and her behaviour is more difficult than others in your class. She has bitten other children, appears incapable of sharing and will not listen to any adults in your classroom. You feel like you cannot control her behaviour and you are now getting regular parental complaints about her behaviour. Amy's parents aren't engaging with you and send other people to collect her.

This is one of those panic moments. You may be feeling pressure from many different places – your classroom staff, other parents and your own thoughts and feelings about pressures on other children, as well as others' perceptions of you. This is one of those 'step back' moments. So let's step back...

Question: Why has Amy moved schools?

Call her previous school and have a general chat with the previous teacher about academic issues. Schools are able to provide this information and will expect this conversation. Ask whether she's on the current SEND register. It will enable you to decipher whether there is an underlying SEND need that has already been identified. It will also enable you to identify whether there is any other agency involvement with Amy, which could lead to you finding out even more information about how to support Amy.

Question: Why aren't Amy's parents engaging?

In terms of Amy's parents, there will be a reason why they don't engage with school, but their support will be vital to progress. You need to use some of the 'Tips on having conversations with parents about behaviour' (Chapter 2). Make them feel at ease by having genuine interactions if you see them on the playground, or phone home to explain that you would like to have a conversation regarding how Amy's settled in at school. Use these invaluable opportunities to engage in developing a relationship with her parents. Again, you may get snippets of information that will help you to support Amy.

Question: Is Amy's behaviour new or has it been apparent beforehand?

When we look at the behaviours of Amy, we can do a Diamond 9. Coming out straight at the top, based on the limited information that we have so far, is the biting behaviours. You would be able to take a proactive and reactive approach to this to ensure there is longer-term change. Firstly, identify that biting is a behaviour that she is carrying out regularly, and communicate this to your members of staff so that they are aware and able to keep an extra eye on this at all times, including non-structured times such as playtimes and lunchtimes. You have that duty of care to the other children, and if she has bitten, then it is your job to make both sets of parents aware. The parents of the 'bitten' child are bound to be upset but reassure them about how you dealt with the situation. The reactive approach involves focusing on changing the behaviours. This may be an intervention.

Practical Strategy – Social story

You may want to use restorative approaches, depending on Amy's understanding of situations, or you may want to tie this into a different intervention. You could use a social story with Amy, discussing biting, like the one here (see **Online Resources**). This is a short, simple description of a specific situation that can be used with children. It gives a child the chance to see what to expect of a situation and alternative choices that he or she could have made. This would need to be read with Amy on a regular basis by a key adult, who could be supporting her through this time.

By pulling in these different strands, a situation that may appear out of hand becomes more tightly controlled. You will have been working on gaining knowledge by speaking to people with prior experience of the situation as well as developing a relationship with Amy, who is new to school and will be dealing with difficulties herself. You will have also been working on engaging her parents and people that are important to her, and tightening your team around Amy. You will have developed a consistent strategy on what to do if the biting behaviours do happen. It will act as an informal risk assessment, so that you are able to provide a support for other members of staff and develop that consistency and calmness in dealing with behaviours. Your SENDCo or behaviour manager may be in the throes of devising a behaviour plan or amending a previous one. On the other hand, you will be supporting Amy in long-term change through your intervention, which will be running alongside all of these actions. Finally, you will also be using your effective communication to alleviate fears in other parents.

When you break down behaviours and situations caused by a child's behaviour, they are much easier to deal with. Sometimes a situation can be so large that you can feel overwhelmed. Step back, break it down and deal with each part in turn. You will feel much more confident tackling these events and, in turn, be more effective in supporting children such as Amy.

Chapter 5
The impact of mental health on behaviour

Disruptive behaviour can be a result of underlying mental health issues. Shocking statistics described by the National Institute of Mental Health show the direct impact that mental health can have on your classroom. At least one in five children will have experienced mental health issues before the age of 11 – assuming that you're teaching a class of 30, then that's six children in your class. These issues can include a range of differing needs that may result in presenting difficult behaviours. Around a third of state-run primary schools in England are able to offer some sort of counselling for children (Department for Education, 2016). This chapter will look at practical strategies that you can take straight into your classroom and that will enable you to support your children's mental health.

Emotional literacy

You can implement activities in a whole-class setting to ensure that you promote positive mental health as a culture in your classroom and even across the entire school.

Idea 1 – Dream jars
Age – *all ages*

Implement – *whole class, individual, small group*

Capitalise on books that are exciting to children; see 'Further reading' for a link to 100 fiction books that children should read before leaving primary school. This example uses Roald Dahl's *The BFG*. Begin by drawing a jar and then open your lesson by discussing the children's dreams for the future. Share the illustrations from *The BFG* to stimulate ideas. Show the children the jar and, for the main activity, ask the children to fill it with their dreams. Children can share this with each other to discuss in further detail. You can have this on display or in a personal file to refer to at a later date.

Idea 2 – Emotion canvas

Age – *all ages but emotions may vary*

Implement – *individual or small group; whole class would work but may have lesser impact*

Choose four emotions – for example: anger, happiness, fear and anxiety. Ask children to draw what these emotions look like. The responses you will get may vary.

Take this a step further: *Discuss words around these that are actually word strings derived from the original emotion, e.g. sad – frown – tears – upset.*

Take this even further: *Ask the children to think about or share with a partner an event in which they experienced this emotion. Offer up one of your own for that two-way trust.*

Idea 3 – Emotion display

Age – *all ages but emotions may vary*

Implement – *whole class*

Print out pictures of different emotions such as happy, sad and excited, or use the ones that your children created during the 'emotion canvas' activity. Display them in a line. Write the name of each of your children on a peg and ask them to attach their peg to the emotion that they are feeling. This can be done during a PSHE session or, even better, at the end of each lesson or transition period. Give yourself a peg! You are part of the class as well.

Idea 4 – All about me

Age – *all ages*

Implement – *whole class at the beginning of the year, individual as part of identity work, small group as part of team-building work*

Decide on what topics you would like the children to share information about. Examples of topics could be family, friends, hobbies, interests, favourite sports, favourite subjects, etc. Make sure that you complete one too so that the information-sharing is two-way.

Idea 5 – This is me

Age – *five to 11 years*

Implement – *depends on adaptation that you are using*

There are two different versions of this activity. The first involves you drawing the outline of one of the children on a big sheet of paper so that you have a base on which to complete the rest of the activity. Children are then encouraged to write what they're thinking in the head part of the diagram (e.g. 'I love school'), what they're feeling near the heart part of the diagram (e.g. 'I feel excited when I meet new people') and their actions in the rest of the body (e.g. 'I love telling jokes and I like to be funny').

The second version is more of an individual approach and needs to take place outdoors. Draw around your child in chalk on the playground. Allow them to complete the above activity using the chalks.

Idea 6 – Problems and reactions

Age – *five to 11 years*

Implement – *individual or small group*

Have two separate areas on paper for your child. Start by talking about a problem yourself that you know the child has had this week and ask your child to discuss it from their perspective. You or the child can note this down or they can draw the scenario. Then discuss the reaction that they had and reflect successes in their actions, or come up with alternative options that they could have looked at.

Idea 7 – Scoot
Age – *all ages*

Implement – *whole class, individual, small group*

The resources that you need are dependent on how many children are playing. This example assumes that there are 30 children in the group. Each child has a 1–30 board, and each child has a number in front of them from one to 30. Deal out 30 scenario cards (examples below). These cards stay with the number.

Children sit either at tables or in a circle. They answer the scenario that is in front of them and write that answer in the corresponding place on their base board. After a minute or so, shout 'Scoot' and they must all move to the next number, taking their base board with them and answering the next question.

It is perhaps best to have true/false, yes/no or one-word answers for speed.

If you are working with a group of children, then reduce the numbers to six or eight or however many there are in the group. The game will be a bit mad and frantic with children moving around everywhere, so first practise moving safely around the group or classroom.

Suggestions for scenario cards include:

- What makes a good friend?
- Is it the truth or a lie?
- Is it likely to happen or not likely to happen?
- Name the emotion.
- How would you feel if…?

Idea 8 – Fascination
Age – *all ages*

Implement – *whole class, individual, small group*

Start your work by explaining the meaning of the word 'fascination' so that children fully understand. Ask the children to then come up with ten fascinating facts about themselves. Children may need support, so model at least one of these facts together – for example, 'I appeared on television when I was eight!'.

Take this a step further: Ask the children to work in pairs and come up with ten fascinating facts about each other, such as 'Jane held the record for the most chocolate cookies eaten in one minute'. You will encourage active listening and promote collaboration, as well as working together towards a common goal.

Idea 9 – What to do when...

Age – *all ages*

Implement – *whole class, individual, small group*

By discussing different emotions explicitly, you can support them as they arise. This activity will help children to become self-aware and able to demonstrate self-efficacy.

Discuss and create a series of resources together, called 'What to do when... you are angry, upset, excited, etc.'. This will allow discussion before children are able to write, draw or create strategies that they can refer to.

Idea 10 – Give me five

Age – *all ages*

Implement – *whole class, individual, small group*

This can be used at a variety of different points during your day. Create a set of 30 A5 'Give me five' cards. You can make them on simple card but laminate them so that they are long-lasting. They can have a range of suggestions on them, such as:

- Give me five ways of calming down.

- Give me five fascinating facts about you.

- Give me five ways of starting a conversation.

This is not only a perfect filler for points in the day when you have unexpected free time – e.g. if you're queuing up for dinner and they aren't ready – but it can also work as a recap of work that you have done in your PSHE time or interventions. Just explain to the children that you have extra time and you're able to play a game for five minutes, then introduce your card.

Mental health as a result of life events

There are a variety of life events that can and will impact on a child's mental health. It is important that, as a teacher, you have some sort of toolkit that will enable you to support the child effectively through this, whether it is a short-term or long-term situation.

Bereavement

According to the Childhood Bereavement Network, up to 70% of the children on your roll will have experienced bereavement. Even more shocking, 92% of children will have experienced a significant bereavement by the age of 16; that's a lot of different emotions for an adult to comprehend, let alone a child.

Children can experience a whole host of bereavements: the death of a loved one; the death of a family pet; a loved one being diagnosed with a terminal illness. Each separate situation will bring a lot of difficult issues, and you may feel ill-prepared and under-qualified to deal with such situations but, as a constant figure in a child's life, you will need to.

When facing one of these situations, you will need to consider the following:

- Acknowledge the changing emotions of the bereaved – the behaviours they exhibit could escalate, children could appear withdrawn, and maybe even stop engaging in conversations, or children could appear exactly the same as they had done prior to the bereavement.

- Avoid assumptions – if children continue to appear happy and unaffected, don't assume that they understand the bereavement.

- Be prepared for a range of situations – not only are you a constant figure for the child, but you are also a constant figure for parents and carers. You may need to be that figure of support for parents too. You will also need to acknowledge differing emotions in adults and not take any negative behaviours personally. Grief is such a powerful emotion.

- Use age-appropriate language – if using euphemisms, be careful of confusing children.

- Provide opportunities for remembrance – always check with parents or carers how they would like you to proceed with dealing with the situation. It is so important that you acknowledge this with the family; they may have very specific ways in which they want the bereavement acknowledged or discussed with their child.

- Consider the impact of events on the wider school community and ways in which you can support them as well.

- Know where to find additional support, e.g. Childhood Bereavement Network.

- Consider the individual and cultural needs of the bereaved.

In terms of language, you need to be mindful of the following:

- Use language carefully, particularly with those with SEND.

- Find out what the child has been told at home so that you can use honest and clear language with them.

- Share information with relevant staff.

- Acknowledge the death when the child returns to school.

- Deal sensitively with incidents of bullying that may arise.

How to support five to eight year olds

- Let the child know that they can talk about their experiences.

- Provide ways to help them express themselves, e.g. writing, drawing, dance, role play.

- Be open and honest. Tell the child if you don't have an answer.

- Avoid statements that imply the grief reaction should be held back.

- Provide fun opportunities for the child to take a break from grieving.

How to support eight to 12 year olds

- Provide a range of opportunities for the bereaved to talk with peers and significant adults.

- Consider providing support to their wider peer group to enable the child's friends to learn how to deal with the situation sensitively and effectively.

- Be aware of challenges that the child may be subjected to, such as the child's first Christmas without their loved one.
- Provide details of external agencies that can provide support.
- Try to reduce other burdens in the life of the child.

Here are some examples of practical activities that you can use with the children to support them during this time.

Idea 1 – Memory book

This activity is extremely useful on a one-to-one basis. It facilitates discussion between you and the child, allowing them to express their thoughts and feelings.

Discuss and complete a variety of activities together, binding them together to make a memory book. Activities could include:

- a picture of their loved one or pet
- favourite activity that they used to do together
- funniest story of them together
- memory stone – you need to collect blank stones and either paint or chalk a memory on one. This can be kept with the child so that they can look it at when they need to.

Idea 2 – Feeling fans

Feeling fans are fans with different pictures of emoticons on. You can print out the resource (see **Online Resources**) and use a split pin to put it together. Show it to the child that you are working with and explain that you would like your child to share the emotion that they are feeling with you, via this fan. With the regular changes in emotion that children feel when going through bereavement, a feeling fan can be an effective tool for them to communicate their feelings. It can be kept on the child's desk and used as a cue for you to talk their feelings through with them, or to ask another team member or peer mentor to support them.

Idea 3 – Paper chains

This is a cheap and simple activity. Make a paper chain as you would normally but, on each chain, write or draw an activity that the child enjoyed doing with their loved one, or a treasured memory. At the end, the child is left with a lovely keepsake.

Attachment

Relationships and learning are shaped by a child's early experiences. So, if we can better understand **WHY** and **HOW** some children behave in the way that they do, we can then find ways to help them enjoy and succeed in life in future.

The theory of attachment was first proposed by John Bowlby, who described it as a 'lasting psychological connectedness between human beings' (Bowlby, 1969, pg 194). He said that children need to develop a secure attachment primarily with their main caregiver in their early years, and multiple attachments throughout their lifespan.

Secure attachments support the mental processes that enable a child to regulate emotions, reduce fear, attune to others and have self-understanding and insight, empathy for others and appropriate moral reasoning. These mental representations are known as the internal working model. Insecure attachments, on the other hand, can have unfortunate consequences. If a child cannot rely on an adult to respond to their needs in times of stress, then they are unable to learn how to soothe themselves, manage their emotions or engage in reciprocal relationships.

A child's initial dependence on others for protection provides the experiences and skills necessary to help a child cope with frustrations and develop self-confidence and prosocial relationships – all qualities necessary for promoting positive engagement with learning. Research has inextricably linked attachment to school readiness and school success (Commodari, 2013; Geddes, 2006).

As a teacher, you will be one of these multiple attachments that is crucial to appropriate development. There are four identified attachment types: secure (*'I'm okay, you're there for me'*); insecure avoidant (*'It's not okay to be emotional'*); insecure ambivalent (*'I want comfort but it doesn't help me'*) and insecure disorganized (*'I'm frightened'*) – Bergin & Bergin 2009; Bombèr, 2007; Geddes, 2006.

It's important to be clear on these different types:

Secure attachment

Securely attached children have experienced sensitive and attuned caregiving. They are able to trust and rely on teachers to meet their needs. As a result, they feel confident in forming meaningful relationships with others, making the most of learning opportunities, engaging in productive activities, problem-solving and exploring the wider world. These children are emotionally resilient and self-aware.

Insecure avoidant attachment

Avoidant attached children have experienced insensitive, intrusive or rejecting caregiving. They appear to be independent of their teachers and seek to meet their needs on their own, as they have not been able to trust or rely on their caregiver. They are task-orientated, self-reliant and high achieving in some aspects but are generally socially uncomfortable, exhibit indifference and avoid close relationships. They may find it difficult to seek help, have limited creativity and may be prone to sudden outbursts.

Insecure ambivalent attachment

Ambivalent attached children have experienced inconsistent and largely unresponsive caregiving. They are easily frustrated and may present as both clingy and rejecting of a teacher, as they seek comfort from but are unable to be comforted by adults. They may present as immature, fussy, helpless, passive or whiney, or they may be angry or petulant. They may also present as attention-seeking and hyperactive and have difficulty recovering from upset.

Insecure disorganised attachment

Disorganised attached children are usually from neglected, abusive and/ or chaotic homes. The child is likely to feel confused by teachers and experience them as frightening or frightened. These children are often highly vigilant, easily distracted, have a strong sense of fear, panic or helplessness and may present with bizarre, extreme, unpredictable or distressing behaviour, which adults may find shocking and difficult to manage. They often present as sensitive to criticism, defiant and/or controlling and are easily overwhelmed.

Children will be presenting in different ways within your classroom, depending on what type of attachment they present. Geddes (2006) discussed how children can present within the classroom.

The insecure disorganised pupil in the classroom

To pupils with such uncertain early experiences, the task that you have set can be an unbearable challenge to their vulnerability, low self-esteem and limited resilience. Their engagement in your task is impaired by mistrust of the adults, an inability to tolerate the humiliation of not knowing and fear of what they do not know.

Their behaviour is led by **omnipotence**, which is their defence against their helplessness, and can display as accusing others of being stupid and useless; the teacher, the task, and others who can achieve can all be the target of their anger and frustrations.

What can you do to ease this?

- Firstly, be mindful that this is not something that you can change but is something that you can support.

- A visual timetable ensures that your child knows what is happening that day and enables you to soothe them through each change.

- Give them some time – little spots throughout the day where you can engage in conversation with your child may ease their mind, even if it's only a little.

Practical activities to support the insecure disorganised pupil

- Interventions need to start with whole-school practices of safety, reliability and predictability. It is only when the child is safe enough and calm enough that we can begin to affect their insecurities through consistent, caring relationships.

- Doable tasks within the classroom are important, and calming actions will be great to use first thing in the morning, particularly as a way of easing into the classroom.

- Children with insecure disorganised attachment may have experienced prolonged absences, and their sense of time and distance can be confused. The use of diaries and calendars in the classroom can begin to establish a sense of dates, times and forthcoming events – especially the endings and beginnings of the week and terms.

- Transitional objects may be useful over the weekend to help with the absences from school, which, over time, will become the secure base and enhance emotional development and thus engagement in learning.

Practical ways to support attachment difficulties

In order to recover from trauma, children need:

- to feel safe and secure physically and emotionally
- relationships and secure attachments
- to be able to express what has happened and is happening.

Successful intervention is based on providing a structured environment with firm boundaries and on nurturing empathic relationships. From this secure foundation, other areas – social skills, self-esteem, emotional literacy, autonomy and self-identity – can be developed. This, in turn, will promote readiness to learn.

Another difficulty that you will face when trying to support children with attachment difficulties is transitions, and this may be another period of time where you face particularly difficult behaviour. It may trigger painful memories of loss or rejection, feelings of high anxiety, fear, grief or even terror. If poorly managed, these changes may lead to a serious setback or trauma. When managed well, a positive experience of change provides a valuable opportunity for learning and recovery from trauma.

With significant transitions (e.g. starting school, changing school, moving up year groups, changes in key staff or attachment figures), the following should be noted:

- The home-school partnership and views of the child are important.
- Transition planning should take place four to six months prior to the transition event.
- Introduce new staff in plenty of time before new beginnings.
- Where possible, the key adult should remain consistent through transitions.
- If the key adults leave or change, it is important to mark goodbyes and prepare the child for the change, perhaps by creating a memory book, card or letter.
- Maintain links after transitions so that the child knows they are 'held in mind'.
- Ensure that information is shared between staff to provide consistency and limit the number of changes.
- When moving schools, create several opportunities for visits by the child and staff.

More practical ways of supporting children with attachment difficulties

Emotion coaching

This is about making children more aware of their emotions and managing their own feelings, particularly during times of difficult behaviour. It will enable you to create a positive learning behaviour ethos and will also enable you to have the confidence to de-escalate situations when behaviour is challenging. During this, you're building internal regulation within the child.

What can you do?

- Teach children/young people about the world of emotion 'in the moment'.

- Give children strategies to deal with ups and downs.

- Empathise with and accept 'negative' emotions as normal (but not the behaviour).

- Use moments of challenging behaviour as opportunities for teaching.

- Build trusting and respectful relationships with children/young people.

Promoting positive mental health

You can promote positive mental health in many different ways within your school. Having a whole-school focus on well-being will be extremely effective in supporting this, and we will cover the subject in the next chapter on well-being. Have a look at the following ideas and check to see whether you are already doing them within school. If not, they are quick wins that you can implement straight away to ensure long-term change for the better.

- Are you teaching positive mental health in your school? If not, look at the ideas in this section, which you can adapt into lesson plans for regular positive mental health sessions.

- Do you have a whole-school approach to mental health? If not, get together in a staff meeting with all members of staff, and discuss the importance that you need to place on positive mental health. Mind map ideas that you can implement and draw up an action plan. The more people that you have on board, the better and more sustainable this positive change will be.

- Are you promoting physical exercise? Ensure that you are teaching your two hours of PE. Implement good behaviour plays, where you simply down tools and go outside for a run around for one minute! Children make the most of their 'free time' and literally zoom around the playground, burning energy and releasing endorphins.

- Are you involving parents and communities in your promotion of positive mental health? Ask local sports people to come in and support your promotion of physical exercise, and ask local restaurants to support you in promoting healthy eating.

- Are you teaching social and emotional skills to your children? You can use simple ideas, such as teaching turn-taking skills during a game of 'Connect 4'.

- Are you discussing positive mental health as a staff on a regular basis? Have a monthly check-in with your colleagues about what went well when you have been teaching positive mental health.

- Are you promoting staff well-being? (More on this in the next chapter.)

- Do you have lines for open and honest communication? Have feelings displays up so that it is a part of daily life, and have a communication box so that children can communicate with you when they don't feel that they can physically speak to you. Can you have a buddy stop in your classroom? Someone for the children to speak to that is a peer?

You are that decisive element in your classroom. If you want to promote positive mental health, then you can! You just need a toolbox. The ideas that I have been feeding into this chapter are the beginnings of your toolkit. Here are some more ideas for you to add to this.

Idea 1 – Can you guess...
Age – *all ages. It will only work with all ages if you differentiate the feelings that the children come up with. Younger children will have limited vocabulary, such as 'sad' and 'happy', and as a challenge you can add in a new word as an introduction.*

Implement – *whole class, groups, individual*

Discuss the words that children know are feelings. Either the children can write them down or you can scribe for the children. Can children show you the emotion, within either their faces or body language, to cement their understanding? Like the game charades, have emotions written down on a piece of paper. Allow one of the children to come up and look at one of the feelings. Without talking, they need to communicate the feeling to the others through facial gestures or body language.

Idea 2 – Expression
Age – *all ages*

Implement – *whole class, groups, individual*

Use the feelings words that you have previously discussed. Remind the children of the ways that they expressed feelings through their actions and/or body language. Explain that they will be portraying the word that they are given through a painting/drawing. Before they start, ask them to discuss the following questions with a partner:

- What colour is your feeling?
- How big/small is your feeling?
- Who feels your feeling?
- What will you need to use to create your feeling?
- How is it different to your partner's feeling?
- What does your feeling look like in you?
- What does your feeling look like in other people?

Idea 3 – Mr Men and Little Miss
Age – *all ages*

Implement – *whole class, groups, individual. Be mindful that it may seem a huge task if you are doing all of the characters.*

Recap on the feeling words, the actions and/or the body language that you used to portray your feelings and the paintings that you created to show your feeling word. Then discuss the *Mr Men* books by Roger Hargreaves. Each characteristic can be linked to a character in one of the books. Explain that, as a class, group or individual, you are going to create a set of characters linked to the feelings. Ask them to discuss the following questions with a partner:

- Is your character going to be big or small?
- What colour will your feeling character be?
- What special features will your feeling character need to have?
- Will your character have a specific texture?
- How will your character be unique from the other characters (feelings)?

Idea 4 – Help!

Age – *all ages*

Implement – *whole class, groups, individual*

Feelings can be a tricky subject and it's important to know who can support you with your feelings. Mind map the feeling that you are focusing on, and create a collage around the word of the people and things that can support the child through this feeling.

Now try this: Role play a situation where the emotion/feeling may arise. Someone else will need to act as the person that you would choose to support and/or celebrate. As a teacher, you can facilitate what action the supportive person does to help.

Idea 5 – Feelings through stories

Age – *all ages*

Implement – *whole class, groups, individual*

Read different picture books that focus on the feelings and emotions that you have chosen. Discuss questions with your child/children, such as:

- Do you like this feeling? Why? Why not?
- Have you ever felt this feeling? When?
- When did you spot this feeling in the story?
- How would we support or celebrate with our friend if they had this feeling?

Now try this: You can do this with musical feelings through song! If you can choose up-to-date songs, then I guarantee the children will engage more!

Idea 6 – Feelings bingo

Age – *all ages*

Implement – *whole class, groups, individual*

Bonus points if you pull in some of the pictures that the children have drawn to create this. You simply need a board of emotions – a different board for each child – and a set of feelings cards. As the bingo caller, you can call out a feeling at a time and, if it's on their board, the child needs to match the feeling word to the feeling picture. The winner is the child who accurately fills their board first!

Idea 7 – How my body feels

Age – *all ages*

Implement – *whole class, groups, individual*

Draw around your body in chalk on the playground. As you discuss the different feelings, ask the following questions:

- Where in our body do we feel this feeling?
- What do our hands do when we feel like this?
- What about our eyes?
- How would our tummy feel?
- What would our breathing be like?

Now try this: Discuss the following phrases and decide what emotion would stir up these feelings:

- hot under the collar
- seeing red
- black cloud
- heart beating rapidly
- tearful
- sweaty palms
- butterflies in your tummy
- knots in your tummy
- lump in your throat
- breathless

- anxiety
- heavy heart
- tired/blank eyes
- trembling knees.

Case study: Lily – aged six

Lily is a child with diagnosed attachment difficulties, and has recently moved to a new school. Her previous school has spoken about her struggles with being able to form attachments with other children, and staff struggled to engage with her. They also report that, although she seemed mature, she couldn't handle playground disputes. She arrives at the new school not knowing anybody and with no transition package in place.

We would like to think that cases like these wouldn't happen but we know that it is a situation that some of you will have already experienced. Be grateful for the information that you have already been given and prepare the intervention straight away.

Allow Lily to have a clean slate in terms of behaviour but be mindful that she is diagnosed with attachment difficulties. There is no choice for her behaviour and she is waiting for the panic to come! Imagine someone circling you with a balloon and a pin. That feeling of panic, knowing that at some point the balloon will burst and it is just a matter of when, is how Lily is feeling right now. It's up to us to support her and enable her to manage these overwhelming feelings.

Ideas to support Lily:

Idea 1 – Key figure

We know that Lily struggles with forming attachments with adults but that does not mean that we give up. Choose an adult that you know will have the patience and experience to work with Lily without taking any of the behaviour that she may exhibit personally. Provide short opportunities for this key worker to start developing a relationship. The beginning of the day and the end of the day should be non-negotiables, as these periods of daily transition can be the most unsettling.

Idea 2 – Emotion coaching

Although we discussed emotion coaching earlier in the chapter, there are lots of different ways in which you can use it. In Lily's case, the key figure could be discussing events during her day and coaching her through the emotions that she is raising, asking and answering key questions to enable her to try to understand the different and difficult emotions that she is presenting.

Idea 3 – Communication book

If appropriate, a communication book could be kept between home and school. Emotions may arise at home that are a result of issues that have happened at school, but where emotions haven't surfaced yet, and vice versa. Remember, knowledge is key and if you have an idea of what might be impacting on behaviour then you can be informed and, in turn, inform your team.

Chapter 6
The impact of well-being on behaviour

It is likely that you will have seen and heard a variety of initiatives to promote well-being. You may have read endless articles and blog posts or engaged in frequent discussions where well-being has been raised. But how much have you have taken on board? Healthy well-being is vital to promoting positive mental health, supporting effective behaviour management and also supporting you in your role. Your well-being is just as important as that of your children. You are that linchpin that not only provides the academic support to enable a child to achieve but also acts in a pastoral role, nurturing and facilitating that social and emotional side to your children. I'm sure that before you trained as a teacher you didn't expect to be so many roles rolled into one.

One of my favourite sayings is, 'I'm a teacher. What's your super-power?'. As teachers, we tend to focus on our weaknesses but no way does that mean that, as a profession, we have low self-esteem. It means that we want the absolute best for our children. By investing this much in our children, we feel every bump, high, dip and surge that the children do, so need to invest just as much in ourselves. If not, there's the genuine worry of burnout. We don't want to lose teachers to burnout when small and simple changes will improve our well-being and, in turn, improve the well-being and outcomes for our children.

There are many well-being advocates in education, all able to spur you on at different points in the year, and some of whom I will talk about further in the chapter, but ultimately it's your job to spur your-self on to be your own well-being champion. Champion your right to positive mental health and advocate well-being in your colleagues. But, before you can champion it, you need to know what it is! It is not just simply being happy but also having self-esteem and self-confidence, being able to work with others and enjoying life experiences.

According to the NHS, there are five different strands that contribute to your well-being:

1. connecting with other people around you

2. being active

3. learning new skills

4. giving to others

5. being mindful.

The practical ideas that follow will have a focus on these different strands, so that you can ensure all bases are covered in your well-being plan.

Well-being week

A well-being week is ideal for covering all of the different strands that contribute to positive well-being. Take a strand each day and have a whole-school focus on it. You can mind map activities with your colleagues and children but here are some ideas that have been tried and tested.

Start your well-being week by having a whole-school assembly (see **Online Resources** for a PowerPoint™ presentation to lead a well-being week assembly) to explain to the children what well-being is, how you want to promote it within the school and how the children can help. Discuss the different strands and explain the focus that you'll be having. Each day, come back to the focus and ensure that you have buy-in from all the staff, so that the children are understanding how to encourage their own positive well-being rather than simply partaking in some activities. Children need to understand that their mental health is just as important as their physical health.

Monday – healthy eating

With this day, you can focus on connecting and being active. Here are some of the activities that you could complete:

Idea 1 – Outside help

Link up with your local community and go into one of your local supermarkets and/or healthy eating businesses. Ask them to support you by providing healthy foods for you to have whole-school tasting sessions or a freebie to take home at the end of the day.

Idea 2 – Make fruit faces

Ask the children to design their own face on a paper plate out of the fruits available. Even better, they can eat it afterwards!

Idea 3 – Fruit smoothies

Bring in some blenders and get your children to design and create their own fruit smoothies for others to taste and rate. Be prepared for questionable tasting sessions!

Idea 4 – Healthy meals

Children could design their own healthy meal that they could share with others. Maybe you could even get your school kitchen or local restaurant on board to vote for their favourite and make it. This provides some fantastic opportunities for community links with your school and local businesses.

Tuesday – self-esteem

With this day, you can focus on connecting and being mindful. Be clear with your children about the meaning of self-esteem as, like well-being, it can be a difficult term to understand.

Idea 1 – 'I am…'

Share cards that are labelled with different words, such as kind, happy, a good friend, helpful, friendly, etc. Children can choose three cards each to describe themselves. This can also have a slight variation and be used in friendship groups. You just need to change the name of the activity to 'We are…'.

Idea 2 – Ask children to bring in a photo or drawing of themselves

Make a class book with these pictures in it. Each member of the class can write a positive comment about each other. At the end, you have a lovely resource to share with the whole class.

Idea 3 – Smile in a circle
Sit in a circle and pass a smile around the circle.

Idea 4 – Self-esteem speech bubble
Children write something that they are proud of, either at home or at school. It could also be something that they are proud of about themselves.

Idea 5 – Superheroes
Get your children to turn themselves into superheroes. Get them to focus on the positive features of their personality and turn them into super powers. They can even design their own costumes.

Wednesday – friendship

This day is your best way of focusing on connecting with yourself and others.

Have a whole day of focusing on friendship and what it is like to be a true friend. Try the following activities/questions:

- Write about your best friend. Children will have someone in their mind who's their best friend.

- Why are they your best friend? The majority of answers may be based around the fact that they are 'kind' and 'nice to them'. You may need to tease out answers that look at commonalities, activities that they do together, good qualities and characteristics that they share.

- How do they support your well-being? This may be a little trickier. Make sure that you have the five strands of well-being up so that the children can be directed in their thinking.

Once the children have more of an idea of the meaning of friendship and an understanding of how friendship can support well-being, you can complete the same activity, but this time thinking about someone that they would like to be friends with.

Thursday – mindfulness

With this day, you can focus on being active, learning new skills and being mindful. One activity that you could complete, which would combine all three, is having a whole-school yoga session. See whether there are any yoga teachers within your circle of staff or parents, and ask them to put on different sessions for each class so that you can ensure whole-school access and participation.

There are also many fun mindfulness activities that you can do with your children:

Idea 1 – Mindfulness colouring
There are lots of free printable colouring sheets on the internet, and I would even recommend that your adults do it too! During time where children are colouring in and concentrating on staying in between the lines, they can remain calm and relaxed and focus on themselves.

Idea 2 – Munch
You'll need to choose what food you want to use but it can be any-thing from crisps to fruit to biscuits. The aim is not just to eat it but to take your time. You need to encourage your children to use their senses before eating it. They need to smell it, look at the colour, feel the texture of it and enjoy every taste and mouthful.

Idea 3 – Body scan
The children can either stand or sit (for comfort, sitting may be pref-erable). Ask the children to close their eyes and think about calming each part of their body at a different time. Start with their heads and ask them to relax their forehead, eyes and nose, focus on their breath-ing, and then relax their mouth and ears. Then you need to guide them down their body, relaxing each part. Once they are at their toes, they need to count down from ten to one and open their eyes slowly.

Idea 4 – Calm walk
Take the children out for a walk around the school grounds. Take the photographic devices that you have within school and ask the children to take a photo of something that relaxes them. They can either write or discuss with a partner why it relaxes them and how it makes them feel. If you have time, instead of taking a photograph, take your sketch books outside and draw the area that is calming for them.

Idea 5 – Balancing

Play some relaxing music and ask the children to do some balances that you lead, whilst you also lead the children in calm breathing techniques.

Friday – healthy body/exercise

On this day, you can focus on being active and learning new skills. This would be a great opportunity to get your PE coordinator on board and ask them to lead sessions for each class. It can be a mini sports day of different obstacles and activities that are easy to differentiate. You can even get your sports leaders on board to help you, so that they can feel a sense of ownership over the day.

You can take this ready-made week and run with it straight away, or replace it with other activities within this chapter or those that your colleagues come up with. It would be perfect if, within this week, you could lead a staff meeting on staff well-being (see **Online Resources**). Ideally, you could start with a word association game to break the ice. Throw some controversial topics in there to really spark the discussion. Ideas that I threw out were: marking, workload, Leicester City, SATs and assessment. Your colleagues will be ready to listen to how you will champion their well-being.

#Teacher5aday

This initiative was launched by Martyn Reah and also has five strands: #connect, #exercise, #notice, #learn and #volunteer. Have a think about these five strands – what do you do currently for each of these? How could you make changes? These strands link into the five strands for well-being but will give you a specific focus.

Ideas on how you can get both staff and children on board for these are as follows:

#connect

This is all about relationships, whether it is developing new ones, nurturing existing ones or connecting with yourself.

Idea 1 – Talk to someone instead of sending a text.

Idea 2 – Send one of your family or friends a letter or a card.

Idea 3 – Speak to someone new.

Idea 4 – Ask a family member or friend how their weekend went and really listen.

#active

This is about keeping yourself active, whether it is physically active or keeping your mind active.

Idea 1 – If you can, walk to work.

Idea 2 – Go for a bike ride or go swimming. If you do this with another person, you can be engaging with #connect too!

Idea 3 – Play your favourite sport or have a game of football with the children.

Idea 4 – Start a staff fitness group. Perhaps get the local Zumba teacher in or even have a staff netball match!

#notice

Being a teacher, your life is constantly busy, and you can be forgiven for missing the calmness and beauty in everyday life. This strand is designed to remind you to note these things and retain them to calm you down in future situations.

Idea 1 – Look at how plants are changing and seasons are moving. See the beauty in each season.

Idea 2 – Take notice of how your friends and colleagues are feeling.

Idea 3 – Take a different route to work or to a friend's house. Notice the differences in the journey and appreciate them.

Idea 4 – Visit somewhere new.

Idea 5 – Look at old photographs of family, friends and even you! Notice the changes over the years. Hopefully this will bring back good memories for you.

#learn

You never stop learning, and new skills enable you to constantly be improving, as well as possibly being an opportunity to link with others.

Idea 1 – Learn something new about your family or friends.

Idea 2 – Read or listen to the news for a week.

Idea 3 – Learn a new dish to cook and cook it for others.

Idea 4 – Do a crossword or a Suduko.

Idea 5 – Research something that you've always wanted to learn about.

#volunteer

Giving to others is always so rewarding, as we already know when we give our time to children. It also doesn't cost anything. There are many different ways that you can support this strand.

Idea 1 – Give somebody a smile.

Idea 2 – Pay a compliment to somebody during the day. We don't necessarily give or receive compliments well, so can you imagine your school culture if you started giving genuine compliments to others?

Idea 3 – Always remember your manners. This may seem really simple but you do so many tasks, and I'm sure that you are supported in so many different ways, that sometimes you may forget to simply pause and say please and thank you.

Idea 4 – Give up your time for somebody, whether it is volunteering at your local charity, doing a sponsored event or helping out at a local fete.

Well-being months

Mike Kerr, an international business speaker on well-being, discussed the possibilities of having themes for each month that have a focus on staff well-being. Some ideas are here for you:

- Characteristic of the month – you could assign the values from your school vision to each week within the month. You could make a certificate and award it to the staff member that has displayed that characteristic.

- Go that extra mile month – offer a prize at the end of the month to someone that you feel has gone above and beyond.

- Healthy eating month – provide fruit in the staffroom for staff to grab on the go during their busy school day.

- What a GREAT idea month – everybody is encouraged to submit ideas that could improve well-being in school.

- Ban month – staff are banned from sending work-related emails before 9am and after 5pm. This will not only enforce well-being for staff receiving the emails but also be a bit of forced well-being on those sending them!

- Walk or bike to school month – you could even link in with national challenges like Bike to School Week.

- Get moving month – climb the stairs, walk during breaks and lunch, jog around the field after school and arrange staff clubs for exercising.

- Appreciation month – make a conscious effort to thank each other in a sincere way.

- Family matters month – this month is dedicated to appreciating and celebrating the staff's families.

- Community spirit month – look for ideas and opportunities to engage with your local community.

- High five month – a whole month of high-fiving whenever something good happens, to remind people to celebrate the small successes.

- Gratitude month – keep a list of things that you are grateful for.

- Clear the clutter month – enough said! Clear out that teacher cupboard!

- Eco-habits month – dedicate the whole month to conserving energy, and make the effort to support others with this too.

- Laugh for no reason month – the power of laughter can be unexplainable and have a huge impact on morale. Have a focus on making people smile and making people laugh!

There are also other initiatives that you can implement, some that do come with a cost, but if you are able to integrate well-being into your school development plan and/or the vision of your school, then you'll be able to either allocate a budget to it or power through a fundraiser that can be allocated to well-being.

Well-being bags

Well-being bags were first developed and shared on Twitter by Abbie Mann (@abbiemann1982), who had set them up as a way of showing her staff how much they are valued. They can be as cheap to make as you like. It's really easy to fill the bags by wandering the aisles at your local pound shops and just scanning for the items that you would like. Some of the things that I've used to fill teacher well-being bags are:

- Popping candy – yes, I know that as soon as you read that, you chuckled, remembering how fun it was to fill your face with the stuff and see how much you could 'handle'. Well, it's still just as fun!

- Whoopie cushions – well, I am just being honest – they are really funny! Watch the faces of your colleagues and you'll soon recognise who is still an inner five year old at heart. I am one of them! Are you?

- Tags – tag each bag with the name of the recipient but, on the other side, have a personal message, such as 'I really value our chats by the photocopier' or 'I really value how you make me a cup of tea when you see that I've been stuck on the phone all lunch'! It's just another opportunity to show people that you've recognised their input and support.

- Speech bubble sticky notes – to write on compliments that they've received so they can keep them or to give someone else a compliment for them to keep!

- Stickers – because no matter what you have heard, no matter how old you are, everybody loves a good sticker!

- Notepad – you can write your awesome ideas down as they flow or write your to-do lists to release the pressure.

- Regular sticky notes – I would be interested to see how many sticky it notes that I use in a year, so an extra pack is always well received and, let's be honest, teachers = stationery addicts.

- Mints – to calm you down during difficult times.

- Biscuits – emergency supply. Keep hidden – you'll end up getting them 'borrowed'.

- Highlighters – similarly to sticky notes, you'll always be grateful for an extra highlighter, and I'm sure that you'll be highlighting key points of this book for later!

- Tissues – for you, for them – regardless of who they're for, there will be a time that you'll need them.

- Sweets – for when you need that support to make it through your 14-hour days – PARENTS' EVENING!

- A stamper – fun, friendly and necessary!

The other version that you would be able to make to promote well-being within your school is a children's version! At particularly stressful times of the year, such as testing or transitions, we need to be mindful of the impact on our children. Well-being bags would be perfect in this situation. Some items are the same as those that go into staff well-being bags. You can differentiate the following ideas to make basic but effective children's well-being bags:

- Notepad – for writing down awesome ideas!

- Sticky notes – write important things on them, use them as bookmarks, use them for reading comprehension answers – the ideas for how to use a them are limitless!

- Highlighters – a pack of mini-highlighters is aesthetically pleasing to the eyes of both young minds and stationery-obsessed teachers.

- ★Freebie alert★ – you can include key aids, such as the RUCSAC method for solving word problems (read, understand, choose (your operation), solve, answer, check).

- ★Freebie alert★ – there are lots of apps and websites that you can use to make motivational posters. It could be a saying that you always use in class or a motivational quote, but it needs to be something that the children will relate to.

- ★Freebie alert★ – there are also well-being apps that you can list and share. Simple apps include an online 'to do' list, relaxation music and a yoga app to link in with the work that you had previously done in your well-being week.

- ★Freebie alert★ – make simple QR codes (there are some great step-by-step YouTube videos!) that link to well-being websites and relaxation tips. If you have a class blog or school website, you can link them to a page that you've already set up.

- Sweets – because, although we always focus on a healthy diet, it's nice to have little treats in moderation. ;-) Well-being as a priority is always a nice reason for a sugary treat!

- A book – you wouldn't think it but pound shops do a great range of children's books at £1 each. This could even be a *freebie alert* if you have a book fair and use the rewards wisely on children's books for your well-being bags!

- A picture of your class/group – because the child that you give this to needs to know that they are never alone. They will always be part of a team – regardless of what happens and the challenges that they face, they will always have their team.

Random acts of kindness

It was only when I was researching random acts of kindness that I realised how much of a global phenomenon it really is. A random act of kindness is something that will have a positive impact on somebody's life, whether it is in the short term or has a lasting impact. It doesn't have to cost you a penny but does need to be something that means something to the recipient. However, the main component is truly knowing when the recipient may need a little light in their life. Similarly to the well-being week, it is a great idea to have a 'random acts of kindness week', which highlights the kindness that I know must be happening in your schools already. I'm going to give you some tried-and-tested ideas that can support a 'random acts of kindness week' within your school this academic year:

- Kindness activity wall – create a display that can act as your wall. Spot the acts of kindness that are shown within your school, note them down and pin them up. Get all of your school staff on board and you'll see a huge variety of kindness. Even get your well-being champions and children involved.

- Kindness jar – write something nice about members of your class or key stage and have some kindness sessions where you can choose one of the slips to read out and celebrate! This works really well for staff too – despite what people may say or what we may think, staff like praise as well!

- Positive sticky notes – use your 'extra' sticky notes from your well-being bags and tag unsuspecting and kind acts within school.

- Catch them being 'good' – provide ideas on a display board of how you can show kindness to one another. Some children can struggle with the understanding of making each other happy so need that little bit of modelling before they can show it. You can link this in to any newsletters or 'kindness' bulletins that circulate within your school. You can even Tweet it! Social media will enable you to share this with parents too!

- Random acts of kindness sheets – create 30 kindness challenges that children can attempt for someone else. These would need to be differentiated, based on what you would be able to attempt, but also need to be free opportunities for children. Make sure that it is optional. Forced kindness is almost as bad as no kindness at all!

- Appreciation postcards – write an appreciation postcard for someone that helps you in school. Try to facilitate children in looking further than simply in their classroom – for example, 'I appreciate how you keep our classroom free from rubbish so that I am free to learn'.

- Motivational videos – find a motivational video to inspire children into completing random acts of kindness for another person to start off your assemblies throughout the year, and not necessarily just as part of this week. Some great, inspirational and kind people to follow on Twitter for random acts of kindness include Action Jackson (@actionjackson) and Shonette Bason-Wood (@shonettebason).

- Class kindness – get each class to share the kindness that they have shown that day or week. You can have a weekly reward for a Kindness Champion based on these submissions.

- Thank-you station – create a writing area in your classroom or school. It can simply be a table with sticky notes, coloured cards, gel pens and glittery pencils on it. Make it exciting! This station is designed to be somewhere that the children can go to write their thank-you notes for others.

Dealing with anxiety

Now, I've given you a wealth of ideas that will enable you to embed ideas for both children and staff well-being. There are also those times when you will need to be able to support children and staff in times of anxiety and crisis. Our first reaction when we see somebody panicked or in need is to say, 'Don't worry!' or 'It doesn't matter'. This may be your reaction but, for your children and even your colleagues, they are worried and it matters to them! However, do try to support your children, as it can be an extremely distressing experience to go through, and to feel alone can be quite scary.

Idea 1 – Talk to your child
Talk them through the experience that is causing them to worry, even if you think that it is you that may have possibly caused them to worry. Use questioning to probe out the problem so that you can talk it through calmly and discuss alternative ways to deal with it.

Idea 2 – Mind map solutions
Ultimately, you want to be able to provide your child with alternative ways of dealing with the situation that they are struggling with but, in order to create self-efficacy, you need to allow them to come up with their own solutions.

Idea 3 – Practise scripts for the situation
When experiencing worries or anxiety, children can go into fight or flight mode. If you are supporting them to deal with a situation, then providing them with a script to use in these situations can be powerful. A script doesn't have to be something that is overcomplicated. It is a short set of steps that children can use to get through an incident of worry or anxiety.

Idea 4 – Joint calmness
When in a period of crisis, children can lose their sense of what to do to calm down. By joining them in calming down, you can be the person to model to your child how to do this. Place your hand on your chest, ask

your child to place a hand on theirs and take deep breaths to calm down. Model deep breathing with the children as well.

Idea 5 – Visualisation
Ask children to think of something that can enable them to relax, whether it is lying on a lilo in the sea and feeling the waves move them up and down or lying in a field underneath the shade of a tree and feeling the wind in their hair and the sun beating down on their face.

Idea 6 – Robot/rag doll
This is a great way to support younger children in relaxation. Ask children to tense their muscles like a robot for 15 seconds and then to flop like a rag doll and relax all of their muscles.

Idea 7 – Reminder
Remind the children that you think they are fantastic! Remind the children of all the things that are fantastic about them and, last but not least, remind them that the class/school wouldn't be the same without them!

Idea 8 – Positivity
Focus on the positives in a situation or within their life. When you radiate positivity consistently, then children will have a script to share positivity themselves.

Idea 9 – Relaxing activities
Once children are out of crisis or you see them beginning to become anxious, divert them with relaxing activities, such as sports, colouring, toy bricks, yoga or painting, or just use it as an excuse to have some fun. Embrace your inner five year old.

Idea 10 – Rewards
If you see a child handling a situation that would usually cause them anxiety, then reward them by noticing it. As we've said before, we shy away from things that we know cause us great worry, so to actually face this is not easy!

Idea 11 – Stay calm

When you see a child experiencing anxiety or worry, it can be distressing for you and your colleagues, but this is the time that they need to see your calmness. If they see you worrying, then they will see more anxiety in the situation. Be mindful of your body language and your own verbal language.

Idea 12 – Resilience

Embed in the children the belief that, regardless of the feelings that they feel, their reactions and how many times that they've had to face anxiety, they have never given up. Demonstrate the importance of this and, if you can, show them. Model situations that you've been in and tell children how you conquered your fear and reached your goals.

Language is powerful in these situations. I've mentioned what not to say but that's not exactly helpful when you're in that situation, so I also wanted to provide you with some helpful sentences to say when a child is worried or experiencing anxiety:

- 'Tell me what you're feeling' – children may not be ready to share their anxiety or have even identified it, but they will be able to tell you how their body is feeling.

- 'How big is your worry?' or 'What colour is your worry?' – this will enable you to have more of an idea of the size of the worry. It can also give you an idea of what strategy or support that you want to provide.

- 'Can you draw/paint it?' – some children really can't find the words to explain their worry or anxiety but are able to demonstrate this through drawing. It will also enable you to discuss it through questioning.

- 'I'm here; you're safe' – when children are feeling out of control, they need some comfort and safety at their peak of worry. If you don't know how to begin, this is a good starting phrase for a child in crisis.

- 'Let's change the ending of this' – with anxiety, you feel stuck in the same circle with the same results, so help them to tell their story and add in alternative endings for them to pursue.

- 'Which calming strategy shall we use?' – give the children a sense of control back to the situation. It will help them to focus on how to end this situation and you'll also be able to weave in some of the strategies that you'll have been providing for your child through intervention.

Implementing ideas that strengthen not only staff well-being but also the well-being of your children will have a direct impact on reducing behavioural incidents within your classroom. This, in turn, will lead to a much calmer atmosphere, where learning can thrive and children can be educated without disruption.

Chapter 7
Interventions

Throughout the previous chapters, I've referred to providing interventions for children that have difficulties in demonstrating positive behaviour within school. However, finding interventions that you can run can be quite difficult because of how varied behaviour can appear. There isn't a magic wand and it isn't as simple as providing one intervention, filling the gap and moving on. Think of it as having the foundations of a house in place, but sometimes different bricks are missing. It's not until you peel away at the foundations that you realise just how many bricks are missing. You have to layer it back up correctly or else the house crumbles.

When you've set up your intervention, you **must** make sure that you choose the right person to deliver it. This may be you, which is not ideal, but if you choose the wrong person, then you could end up regressing further.

Qualities that they must have

- able to separate the behaviour from the child
- able to form relationships quickly
- able to understand that behaviour is communicating something
- want to support children with behaviour rather than punish them and end it there.

I am not saying that these are the *only* four qualities that they must have but they are vital and the member of staff must know that they are part of the support and subsequent change. Your communication with them needs to be clear, supportive and regular, as it needs to be tight if you want effective and ongoing support.

Once you've chosen your member of staff, they want to be part of the change and your child understands what they are working towards, you're going to need some ideas for intervention. It would be really easy for you to get schemes of work or prewritten interventions and run with them. I'm not discounting that but, to be really effective, you need to pick and use appropriate parts of each to create an intervention that is focused on the needs of your child. You have a wealth of ideas within this book that you can put together to create a six-to-eight week intervention. Grab your highlighter, go through the pages and highlight the first six to eight that you will use. More than one child? No excuses. I'm pretty sure that they do other colours! Grab another and get highlighting.

Interventions to support children with feelings, empathy and self-esteem

The following ideas for intervention will focus on looking at feelings, empathy and self-esteem. I will tag them so that you can clearly identify which ones you will need.

Idea 1 – Superhero
Self-esteem

Discuss what it means to be a hero. What do we think a hero is? What makes them a hero? Do heroes need to be famous? Is your hero famous? Are there heroes in daily life – for example, firefighters, police officers, teachers, dinner ladies? What qualities do heroes have?

Draw your hero and label their qualities.

During the activity, ask the children whether they possess the qualities that they are identifying. Tease out whether they think they are capable of developing these qualities if they don't think that they have them already. How will they do this? Why is it important to constantly strive to improve ourselves as people?

Idea 2 – Change it up!
Feelings, self-esteem

If the child/children could change anything, whether it be emotional ('I wish I could stop myself from getting angry so quickly'), practical ('I wish that I could learn to ride my bike without stabilisers') or imaginary ('I wish that I was Wonder Woman'), what would it be?

Children can choose three things and create them, either with modelling clay, through painting a picture or through you taking a photograph of them completing a freeze frame.

Discuss with your child what can actually change and what can't. Think about how they can work towards changing this, whether it is through smaller steps or something that you can support them with, such as learning to ride a bike. Don't limit what you can do in an intervention. If their goal is to learn to tie their shoelaces, help them.

Idea 3 – Positive experiences
Feelings, self-esteem, empathy

When working with a child who can appear quite negative and self-deprecating, it is always nice to start on a positive experience. Talk to the children about occasions. Before I continue, just make sure that you have a child's history before completing this, as we can't assume that all children celebrate or have a positive home life where they do celebrate. Ask the child/children what the best present that they have ever received was. Why was it the best? How did they feel when they received it? How did they feel when they opened it? How did they express this to others?

Use a cardboard box to create a present. Make it as appealing as possible. Ask the children to put the feelings (perhaps written on card) inside them. As you pull them out, children could act out the feelings.

To extend this further you could add in the feeling of disappointment. What would they do if the present was disappointing?

Idea 4 – Life journey
Feelings, self-esteem

Ask children to recall experiences that they have had since birth. You can write them all on sticky notes. Once you've completed them, ask the children to put them in order – from birth to now. You can then ask the children to discuss which events they think were the most important in their life (no more than five). Take each event and discuss the feelings that come when they think of this event – why? They may be positive or negative feelings. They may even be events that they know were important but don't remember!

This could be quite a big piece of work that you are doing with your child, and may span over a few sessions. You could extend this even further by asking them about important events that they think will happen in the future, such as moving into the next school year, eighteenth birthday, etc. Discuss about how they think they'll feel in the future about these life events.

Idea 5 – Dragon's Den
Feelings, self-esteem

A perfect activity to do with children when you want them to start thinking about what they could achieve. Ask children to imagine that they have a business. What do they think that they could sell or what skill could they utilise? What would the name of their business be? Would they have a partner or would it be theirs solely?

Ask them to create their own business logo. Whilst they are doing this, you could ask them how they would have to act as a business owner. What qualities would their partner need to have, if they are having one?

Afterwards, you could ask them if they really think they'd own a business in future life. Why? Why not? What would they like to do when they're older? Share your experiences of what you wanted to be as a child. This is the funny part, as my children never believe that I always wanted to be a teacher!

Idea 6 – Celebrations
Empathy, feelings

Start with asking your child if they have won anything before. Ask them to paint/draw someone else that has won a prize. How do they think that they feel? Introduce the word 'pride'. Have they ever felt proud of someone else? Have they ever made someone proud? If you get a resounding 'no', then come up with a time that the child has made you proud. Remember that you don't necessarily have to win something to feel proud.

Lead on to discussing winning. Do you always have to win? How do you react when you win something? Role play a scenario of winning something. What should you do? What qualities should you choose? Introduce the word 'boasting'. How would other people feel if you boasted about winning? How would you feel? Have you ever been in this position?

Idea 7 – Shaking tablet
Feelings

You can adapt this onto paper if you don't have access to this technology.

Ask children how they watch TV and/or films. Explain that you will be exploring the feeling of fear today. What have you seen on TV that has made you scared? Draw your scary vision onto the tablet/paper – is it real or is it pretend? Discuss the difference between real and pretend? What scares you more – something that is real or pretend? How does it make your body react – for example, sweaty palms, fast-beating heart?

Ask children to discuss the last 'real' thing that they have been scared of. How can we prepare ourselves for fear? What can we do? Are all fears 'bad' fears? For example, with a fear of fire, the fear keeps us safe! Ask children to draw a magic finger to switch off the fear!

Idea 8 – There's not just me in the world
Empathy

Draw four characters of various ages – for example: toddler, teenager, adult and elderly person. What do you think that their dreams in life are? What do you think that they dream about at night? Create a dream for each character.

Whilst the children are completing this activity, tease out during questioning what their different hopes in life might be. What may be their important memories?

You could even go a step further and ask them to discuss the dreams of an inanimate object. The level of difficulty for this challenge is even higher, as they will have no experience of this and won't be able to relate to it at all!

Idea 9 – But why is he so sad?
Empathy, feelings

Show the child/children a picture of a sad child. How is he feeling? How can you tell? Ask them to draw what they think the child is think-ing about. They can write this if they would prefer. Discuss how to be a good and active listener. What can you do with your body language to show someone that you are listening? Practise this.

Ask the children what questions are useful when somebody has a problem and how they can use this to support someone that is sad. For example, 'I can see that you look sad. Would you like to talk to me?'

To take this a step further, the children could act out the problem that they created earlier, with your chosen child being the 'listener'. This means that they can practise the questions and body language that you had teased out earlier.

Idea 10 – Who would be friends with a robot?
Feelings, empathy

Show the children a picture of a robot. Would you be friends with him on the playground? Why? Why not? Do you think other people would be friends with him on the playground? Tease out how you think that he may feel, being so far away from his family. Why do you think that this is?

Draw new friends for the robot. What games do you think that he'd like to play? How do you think that he feels now?

Take this a step further and ask the children whether they have ever felt lonely or excluded from a group. Discuss this.

Extend this even further by creating a 'guide to this planet that we call Earth'. Can you draw the robot's school in futuristic times? What are the similarities and differences between their school and the robot's school?

Interventions to support children with anger

Anger can be a really difficult emotion to recognise in yourself before the 'eruption'. It really is something that you need to support your children to recognise within themselves so that they can begin to become responsible for their own emotions.

Idea 1 – My hot spots

Are your children able to recognise their own hotspots and what gets them heated? If they struggle to know what gets them angry, then give them a simple scale of 1–5 or 1–10 and ask them to rate a series of events that happen in their lives such as:

- somebody taking the last pencil
- another child bumping into them
- not going first for dinner
- getting called a name
- PE
- knowing that they're going to an afterschool club
- being asked to tidy up.

Idea 2 – Pouring cold water on the fire

This session can usually come after the previous one, as it leads in quite well. You can discuss which of the scenarios have the highest rating for you. Ask your children whether they have their own ways of calming down when they are angry. You can note these strategies down. Discuss with the children what is the most effective.

Share the following list with the children:

- counting back from ten
- breathing deeply
- imagining that they are holding something cold
- stiffening all of their muscles and then relaxing them
- visualisation – think of somewhere that calms them and visualise themselves there.

Have they tried any of these strategies? How would they rate them? Which would be most/least effective?

Ask them to think about all of the strategies that they came up with, as well as the ones that you presented, then come up with the most effective strategy so far. Leave the session by coming up with a strategy that they are going to try in the coming week.

Idea 3 – Anger diary (see Online Resources for an outline for an anger diary)

Introduce the 'anger diary' to the child during your session. Ask them to use the scale to measure their anger on a daily basis or lesson-by-lesson basis if you are able to support and remind them to do so.

This will allow you to reference particular days and incidents during your intervention sessions. You could also have options for different emojis to allow children to represent other emotions that they had other than anger, such as frustration or feeling upset. You could also have a section for strategies used and their rating of them.

Idea 4 – Express yourself

Discussing anger can be seen as quite aggressive, as usually children are in a heightened state when they attempt to express themselves, so communicate with your colleagues what you are trying to achieve with your child so that they know to expect this kind of communication when the child is first starting to try to communicate.

When aiming with the child for them to communicate when and why they are angry, you're aiming for the following key principles: keeping calm when you communicate how you feel, expressing yourself and your feelings without being disrespectful if another party is causing your anger, and offering an alternative solution if you feel that there is one. Always communicate to the child and/or instil in them that it is okay for a child to speak to an adult and say, 'I am feeling angry and I need your help to calm down'.

Idea 5 – Angry mind, angry body

You may have previously discussed the effects that being angry has on your body. Make a set of emotion posters with the children. Start with 'When I am angry this happens to my body' and list the effects that it has on the child. If they are struggling to communicate how it affects their body, you can discuss possible ways that it may appear through their body, such as:

- sweaty hands
- dry mouth
- headache or tension within their temples
- gritting of the teeth or jaw ache
- making fists with their hands or scratching their arms to soothe themselves
- tightness in body/muscles
- being fidgety or wanting to pace

- thumping heart
- their angry thoughts overpowering their mind, instead of being able to listen to things that people are saying to them
- feeling heated, going red or trembling
- raising their voice
- breathing quickly or feeling teary

Together, come up with some strategies that you can use for calming down when children feel this way. Feel free to use some of the relaxation ideas that I mentioned in the well-being chapter.

Idea 6 – How do people see me?

Do the children know anybody that gets angry? How do they feel when they see someone else get angry? How do they think people feel when they see them get angry? Teachers? Other children? Mum and Dad?

You can be as creative as you like with this activity but, throughout the session, you need to tease out answers to the following questions:

- What three words would you use to describe yourself?
- What three words would your teacher use to describe you?
- What three words would your best friend use to describe you?
- Are there any qualities that you'd like to have?
- What's your best quality?

Idea 7 – Anger thermometer

Note 5-10 things to make you angry. Write each one on a sticky note. Place them into three categories: 'annoy me', 'make me heated' and 'really anger me'. Discuss which physical symptoms they would feel if one of these situations happened. Put them into order, from the situation that would anger them the most to the situation that would annoy them the least.

Link these situations to strategies that would support them. Discuss how they need to be aware of the situations that appear further up the thermometer – can they avoid these situations? Can any measures be put into place to support them with this?

Idea 8 – I can't do it/yes I can

Think of a situation that you have been in where you have felt that you can't do something. Does this make you angry? What would you tend to say? Pick out language that you may use, such as 'I can't do it!', 'Everyone thinks that I am rubbish' or 'I will fail'.

Make a table and put all of these negative comments into it. With a partner or alone, if your child is good at communicating, come up with positive alternatives, such as 'I may not be able to do this straight away but I will be able to because I am resilient and determined', 'Everyone knows that I try hard' or 'I can do this'.

Create motivational posters to put up and support not only the child who may be struggling with their self-esteem here, but also the class, who will benefit as well!

Idea 9 – I can think about this differently

Look again at scenarios that will cause them to feel angry – someone bumping into them, someone taking the last pencil, and so on.

Ask children what they think at the time – other children are targeting them, someone is stealing their pencil, etc.

Discuss what the children feel when they are in a calm mood about these situations – 'the child probably tripped over and didn't mean to barge into me' or 'there aren't enough pencils on the table and I need to let the teacher know!'.

Idea 10 – Don't be an Angry Bird

This can be any theme that will grab the attention of your child.

Discuss the child's effective strategies for cooling down. Create a set of posters using an interest that the child currently has to illustrate them. Label each one: When I feel … (my palms getting sweaty, etc.), I … (breathe deeply and count from five to one, etc.). This will form either a set of posters to display or a lap book that children can have in the drawer or locker to use when they feel themselves bubbling.

ADHD interventions

ADHD can be a controversial diagnosis. When you speak to people, there are a whole range of opinions over how to support a child with ADHD effectively. Some children with ADHD are medicated but you shouldn't consider this to be problem solved. You need to be running interventions alongside medication, if this has been the route taken, so that the children can develop coping strategies as well. ADHD is a common and complex neurobiological condition, which significantly interferes with everyday life for your child. It is often inherited and has different levels, which can often be masked if you have multiple people in the family living with ADHD.

For a successful diagnosis of ADHD, a child needs to present the following traits: inattentiveness, hyperactivity and/or impulsivity.

Inattentiveness

Children need to present six of the nine criteria:

- rushing that leads to careless mistakes, e.g. errors in their work
- struggles to pay attention in tasks or during play activities
- often does not appear to be listening when you are talking directly to them
- fails to finish work or instructions but not through defiance
- struggles to organise themselves, tasks, etc.
- reluctant to engage in activities that require effort
- loses things that are required for a task, e.g. pencils, rulers, etc.
- easily distracted
- appears forgetful during daily life.

Hyperactivity

- child often fidgets
- child leaves seat or cannot cope in situations where being seated is expected and/or required
- often runs around and climbs – what the children do often appears as dangerous to an adult in a situation
- has difficulty in engaging in games and situations quietly
- is always 'on the go'
- is perceived as a chatterbox and is nearly always talking.

Impulsivity

- blurts out answers without putting their hand up – again, this isn't an act of defiance
- struggles to take turns
- often interrupts people and barges in on their games.

Children with ADHD have no control over these reactions, but we can support children in developing strategies to try to prevent these behaviours from appearing so often. A child with ADHD needs you to be supportive, positive and most definitely have a good sense of humour. Those that work with children with ADHD – and it's up to you to model this – need to accept that a child with ADHD will demonstrate behaviours that will impact on daily life within school. They must be flexible about delivering lessons (as concentration will be low), stay close to the child so that they can support them to stay on task and, finally, keep eye contact whilst giving short and clear instructions to the child. To support a child with ADHD effectively, you and your colleagues need to be consistent with rewards and boundaries for a child.

Adapt your classroom to support children with ADHD

- Arrange the classroom and consider your seating plan so that your child is away from as many distractions as possible.
- A visual timetable will provide your child with structure and will help them to realise and see the boundaries of the day.
- Be clear on your rules of the classroom. Keep them short, sharp and clear.
- Be flexible in delivery of lessons. Use different media to engage your child such as computers, art and physical activity.
- Provide your children with the equipment that they will need for the lesson. This supports a child who may experience disorganisation but also limits time for distraction.
- Use visual prompts to communicate to the children if they need to be aware of their fidgeting, level of noise, etc.

- Allow the child to take frequent but structured breaks.

- Play soft music during your lessons. Classical music works well for calming the levels of noise within a classroom.

- Have a quiet area for your child to visit if they need to get away from group work, as it may be causing too much distraction.

- Break tasks down into short instructions.

- Encourage children to be back on task through simple prompts, such as a hand on the shoulder or a finger on their work. You do not need to verbally bring children back onto task or else you run the risk of bringing too much attention to a situation.

- Use genuine and specific praise when a child is on task.

- Reward work completed in the time allowed, whether it is a sticker on a chart, a housepoint, or another form of reward.

- Be sensitive to the environment. Do not underestimate the negative effects that wind, hot weather and Fridays(!) will have on your child's concentration and work output.

- Provide a fidget-buster, e.g. tangle, sticky tack, stress ball.

Lego™ Therapy

Lego™ Therapy was developed by Dan LeGoff in 2004 and is mainly pitched as a social development programme for children with ASD. Simon Baron Cohen and Gina Gomez have researched it and both recommend it. It's a collaborative play therapy, where children work together to build Lego™ models. To be able to access this intervention, you need to work on joint attention, shared goals, verbal communication and mutual purpose. It can be differentiated by equipment. It can also be used as a team-building exercise to help work on adult communication!

Lego™ Therapy is one of the very few strategies where research has proved significant improvements in social competence at the end of intervention, as well as at a later follow-up. It is said to be suitable for children aged six to 13, but we have used it with children aged four to six, with the Duplo™ sets. It is for use with individuals and small groups (no more than three). It is perfect for use in social skills groups, or in lunchtime or after school clubs but, again, choose your member of staff wisely or it can just descend into a regular Lego™ club and lose its impact straight away.

Lego™ Therapy measures social competence through three components:

1. motivation to initiate social contact with peers
2. ability to sustain contact with peers for a period of time
3. overcoming aloofness and rigidity.

You'll be targeting and developing the following skills with your children: joint attention, collaboration with others, sharing, turn-taking and joint problem-solving skills.

As the observer, you will be able to take notes on how your child is performing in the following areas:

- Communicating ideas – throughout this intervention, communication will be vital for success, and it's often a skill that the children find the hardest as they can be quite focused on themselves and their needs. Developing that awareness of others will be a key focus.

- Taking account of others' ideas – it really does develop that true sense of teamwork. The final product will be a culmination of all of the ideas from the team.

- Compromising – when taking account of others' ideas, your child will be developing the skill to compromise. Some will need support in this and you'll be able to spot this.

- Showing and taking account of others – the intervention will not work without the teamwork element, whether it is you and the child or a group of three working on a project.

- Thinking about the good points of others' ideas – children will need to evaluate the ideas of others to choose the strongest points and move forward.

- Dealing with competition – there will be an in-built sense of competition for the child(ren) to simply finish their Lego™ project within the time of an intervention. It will be your job to identify frustrations and support children in staying calm so that they don't make unnecessary errors.

What is your role?

- Facilitate – you need to provide the Lego™ sets. They need to be the project sets and not simply boxes of Lego™. I've found that the Creator™ sets (3-in-1) are perfect for children aged seven to 11, and the Duplo™ sets are great for children aged four to seven.

- Support the children in setting the rules for the group sessions, and you also need to be the lead person to revisit them at the beginning of every session. It may also be useful to visit them at the end of the session to make sure that you all agree that the sessions have run smoothly and they have been working within these parameters. These rules need to be made by your group but, essentially, be as follows: build the models together; if you break it, then you need to fix it; if someone else is using a piece, then you cannot just take it and you must ask first; use your indoor voices to communicate with others; only use polite words and positive language with your team; and tidy up at the end. All of these rules must be followed to consider the intervention to be successful. It doesn't matter how many steps have been completed in a session as long as these rules have been followed.

- Prompt the children to partake in joint problem-solving when they are struggling.

Once you've chosen a Creator™ set or Duplo™ model, open the pack and you will find a set of visual instructions. This is your plan for the lesson. There are three roles in the group: builder, engineer and supplier. The builder is the child that takes the bricks from the supplier and builds the model. The engineer is the only person that can see the visual instructions and instructs the supplier which bricks they need. They cannot point to what they need and must describe them. The supplier is the person that finds the bricks and hands them to the builder. There are lots of free resources on the internet to allow you to provide badges to each of your children, visual rules for your group, and much more.

There is a clear and definite progression through Lego™ Therapy: levels one, two, three and four. Children need to progress through the stages to complete the intervention. For some children, intervention can be short but for others it can be longer, with extended times stuck on each stage working on different skills. There is no set time on each level.

Level One works on a one-to-one basis and will simply be your child working with another adult. As there are only two people in the intervention, you won't be able to use all three roles during that time. The child acts as the builder and the adult needs to take on the roles of both engineer and supplier.

Level Two is the introduction of one other child. The child must be well chosen; somebody that doesn't struggle with communication and social skills. At this stage, you can each have a role.

Level Three is where all three roles are taken up by children and you sit back as observer.

Finally, Level 4 is free choice. Children still need to take three roles but the roles alternate (led by you) during the intervention time, so that children are able to have a go at each role. They also have free choice on what they make, so you can leave the Creator™ sets and simply provide a box of Lego™. You still need to lead the topic – e.g. 'build me a castle' – but the design idea is up to the children. Be aware that, with the change in roles, the model will change and children will need to be able to deal with compromise and other people's ideas.

I'm sure that you'll be able to find some ideas that you can use within your intervention throughout this chapter, but don't forget the basics of intervention: plan, deliver, assess and review. When you stick to this cycle, the impact will be evident and, in turn, minimise disruptive behaviour within your classroom.

Chapter 8
The impact of relationships on behaviour management

Relationships are a huge influence on moving forward and having success with positive behaviour management. It isn't only the relationships with our children that are integral but also the relationships that we have with all of our school staff. I continually talk about the team around a child, but it's pivotal. A child needs to feel like they really are a linchpin within your school – and they are! This means that positive behaviour management is everyone's business and shouldn't just be left up to you. We see so many teachers who feel like the behaviour of their children is ultimately down to them. A few more feel like they can ask for support from their classroom support staff and their SLT but, if you actually speak to other staff within your school, they will be more than happy to become part of the team around the child.

Sometimes, when you need to have a breather from a tense time, it's nice to have another member of staff in school that you can send your child to go and take a note to. Just widen this circle. For example, send a note to your school business manager (SBM) and then, later on in the day, you can go and talk to your SBM and casually ask how your child has been. In developing this relationship, you are widening the circle further; your SBM will start asking how your child is getting on and begin to develop a relationship with the child, whom they previously may not have seen.

The following ideas can support you in developing a relationship with your child, but they can also be passed on to your other school staff to use.

Idea 1 – Getting to know you

Get a plain A4 piece of paper and split it into four. Ask the child to come up with something that they want to talk about, such as a TV series, football, etc. You then write something that you want to talk about. Do this twice so that all four spaces are filled – two by you and two by the child.

Then take each conversation starter and discuss. By the end of the session, you can assume that you may be discussing their two favourite topics, so you will know more about them. But relationships are mutual and you may also have shared your two favourite topics. It's important to remember that it's a given that you will invest yourself in a child but they need to trust and invest in you as well to build a relationship.

Idea 2 – Two truths and a lie

It's likely that you've played this game before but, just in case, I'll explain. You have to come up with three facts about yourself: two must be correct and one needs to be a lie. You can say them in any order but don't give away the lie! After you've said your three facts, the other person needs to guess which one is a lie. It's designed to just have some fun with your child; although you will be finding out two facts about them, it's nice to just have some laughter together.

Idea 3 – This is me!

Create a representation of yourself; you could create a poster but you may want to be even more creative, by making a YouTube video about yourself, a slideshow, a news bulletin, etc. Your child should do the same. Within your representations, you could include answers to questions, such as:

- What is your favourite food?
- What is your biggest fear?
- If you could be a film, what film would you be?
- What is your superpower?

Your facts will change depending on the time of year at which you are reading this book. If it's at the beginning of the year, then you are just starting to develop the relationship, but you may be in the situation where you are forging a relationship after a period of difficult behaviour. You may even be looking at these ideas to try to repair broken relationships. These activities are ideal for all of these situations, as you're not having to act as the person providing boundaries, rules and consequences; you are simply having fun getting to know your child.

Idea 4 – Show and tell

Three words that make teachers shudder to their very core and their eyes roll: 'show and tell'. But the children absolutely love showing you the pet rock that they found on the way to school or their special piece of fluff, which they've kept all morning to give to you. These things matter to our children. They are proud of them. During these times, you get to really develop the relationship with your child outside of school. If they share the medal that they won at a football tournament, you could use this to ask them on a Friday whether they have a big match coming up. You can either do it on a whole-class basis or you could add it to the last ten minutes of your intervention sessions.

Idea 5 – Behaviour Jenga®

This is a fun and lively way of engaging children, and is a spin on a family favourite game that the children may already have played.

All you need to complete this activity is an old Jenga® game, coloured stickers and the Jenga® cards template (see **Online Resources**). You can adapt the Jenga® cards to suit your context and the age range of the children. Use your coloured stickers and put one colour on each Jenga® block. I found my stickers from the local pound shop. Add coloured stickers to each of the cards but make sure that you have enough cards with matching Jenga® blocks!

You play Jenga® in the regular way, taking turns and sticking to the Jenga® rules. Once the first player has removed one of the blocks, look at what colour sticker you have. If it's red, then take a red card and so on. The children will be presented with a scenario and they need to answer in the correct manner to gain the number of points on the card. Then it's player B's turn and so on…

It's your choice whether you actually keep track of points or play non-competitively. You may want to change it from points to house points or merits, etc. Be prepared for lots of laughter!

Relationships with parents

To cement relationships with children, it is important to continue to develop your relationships with parents. Regardless of any difficult conversations that you may have had in the past, you need to make sure that your experiences are as positive as possible. Always smile. If 90% of your engagements with parents are positive, then you are more likely to have the good relationship that you need to move forward and support the children. Have an ongoing dialogue with parents and remember to highlight the positives of the day – for example, 'Jessie produced some fantastic writing about the Vikings; have you seen it?' Another great way of developing a meaningful relationship with a parent is asking questions about the child that you genuinely want to find answers to – for example, 'What is their favourite thing to do outside of school?' Or you could share observations: 'She absolutely loves "Spag Bol Tuesdays" – what's her favourite food at home?'

You can ensure that your communication with the child's parents/carers (and all of your other parents) is effective by being mindful of the following:

- Varied communication – I appreciate that you have a busy life in school but it is better if you ask to know the best method of communication for you to use to relay messages to parents. If you use this preferred method of communication, then you are more likely to receive regular dialogue and have more support.

- Time – when there is an issue, you should contact the child's parents as soon as you have the full information. If you wait, you run the risk of second-hand information reaching parents, and we all know how disastrous that can be. It can cause unnecessary bad feeling and awkward situations. Also remember that it is two-way. When parents have contacted you, make sure you reply the same day, even if it is just a simple phone call acknowledging their message before you investigate an incident further.

- Consistency – if you are part of a job share or there are more staff in the classroom – such as cover supervisors or LSAs – then all must be clear on what is happening. A communication book is a good idea to enable all to be aware of any incidents. Communications must also be frequent from all members of the staff involved with the child, so that it does feel like a positive relationship.

- Honesty – there is no point in sugar-coating messages as, again, it will be worse in the long term. As a teacher, you want to see that everyone follows through with what they say. For parents, it is exactly the same thing. They want to see that you truly want to investigate incidents, have an active interest in their child and also deal with what you say you will – so just make sure that you do.

- Clear communication – be clear and concise when you communicate with parents. Stay away from the use of acronyms or at least explain them if you do need to use them.

Mood hoovers

There is bound to be a 'mood hoover' in your team at school. It's okay to admit it – maybe you're the mood hoover, but I doubt it seeing as you're reading this book to try to improve your positive behaviour management. A mood hoover is exactly as it sounds: a killjoy, a fun sponge, someone who sucks out the positivity from absolutely everything. When you fire off an idea in a staff meeting, it's that person who shoots out, 'This definitely won't work. We've tried it before. Failed'. The really ingrained mood hoovers won't even speak; they will just scoff at your contributions. They will also be those who come out with helpful contributions like, 'Oh yes, little Marie. She's been a nightmare since she started. They've never changed her. They never will. Just sit her out of your class and focus on the rest of the children.' See what I mean now? Is a picture forming in your head of the mood hoovers in your school? I knew it!

So now you've identified your mood hoovers, we're going to bring some positivity to their lives. You never know – they may even end up making you a cup of tea when you've had a difficult day with little Marie.

Idea 1 – Don't avoid them

There is a lot of advice about mood hoovers that starts with the word 'avoid' but I don't think that you should. Continue to talk to ALL members of staff and be positive. Model a positive attitude that embraces change and other people's ideas. We all get nervous of change and new ideas, so it may be simply nerves that stop people from embracing difference.

Idea 2 – Get them involved

Find out their strengths and positives and embrace them. Put them to good use and involve them that way. When they see the change that can result from their input, then you're more likely to get positivity from them.

Idea 3 – Short-term wins

Linked to the point above, you need to make sure that you purposely build in short-term wins. Those that you consider to be mood hoovers will see the success that your children are achieving, and actually see a purpose in supporting you.

Idea 4 – Talk

Some mood hoovers don't even realise that they are being negative – it can just be a destructive circle that they find themselves in. When they make negative comments, just speak to them and ask for their support. You may find that they change their perspective and attitudes when they realise their impact on the moods of other people and situations.

Circle of Adults

The 'Circle of Adults' was devised and developed by Newton and Wilson (2006). It is a deep approach that enables you to reflect upon incidents and individual children but also provides a problem-solving session. By using a team approach like this with a wider group, you are able to come up with longer-term solutions that have an impact on your children.

I'd recommend that, if you are dealing with a particularly difficult situation, you need a diverse team so that you can have all different angles seen in the situation. This will enable you to really consider the best ways forward and, ultimately, the best outcomes for the child.

Using the diverse team, regular meetings need to be held. All of the members of the team need to have the child's future and well-being at the forefront of their minds. Make sure that all of the team are aware that it will more than likely be an emotionally charged session. There are many emotions shared during the sessions, including personal feelings and opinions, reactions from discussing emotional incidents and confidential information about the child being shared, some of which may be harrowing. These sessions are extremely powerful and provide a support network.

How do the sessions run?

- Always welcome the members of team. Discuss the reasons behind calling the group together and the values that you want to provide. Reinforce the reasons why you continue to support children with challenging behaviour, along with the need for understanding, inclusion and reflection.

- Facilitate introductions amongst the group. If it is your first session, then you need to establish some ground rules for the session. Reinforce them for every other meeting. Then clarify the aims of the session.

- Open up the forum of the group and ask for the issues that people have experienced since you last met. You may need to prioritise which area of concern it is that you will be focusing on during this session.

- The presentation takes place; the member of the group who raised the concern is asked questions to enable them to share the child's background up to this point. Another member of the group (identified at the beginning) will be recording the key themes emerging on a large piece of paper where all can see it. That person will also be summarising the overall picture that will be emerging. The class teacher of the child needs to be in charge of keeping a clear focus on the child and their situation. It is also their job to keep out judgment, generalisations and inaccuracies. Pull out the positives and negatives about the child's behaviour – not about them. Probe further – what does it feel like to be this child? How do they feel when you discuss their behaviour with them?

- Whilst this presentation is happening, another member of the team (chosen at the beginning) should be listening intently and preparing themselves for subsequent discussions from the child's perspective. After the presentation, the facilitator asks this person ('the child') how they are feeling about what has happened so far.

- Other members of the group may have questions about the pupil – the facilitator needs to take these at this point so that they can be discussed.

- Describe the actual process of a relationship. Discuss with the teacher how they have developed their relationship so far. How would a fly on the wall see your relationship? If we could see you together, what would we see? What would it be like?

- Discuss previous relationships that the child has had. Have these experiences been positive or negative? Ask the teachers whether they've had any relationships that may impact on their treatment of the child. Have they transferred any of their past relationships onto their relationship with the child – for example, has your own child behaved like this? Did you behave like this? By exploring this possible transference, the group can explore whether there may have been roles transferred onto the teacher by the child, such as the role of a parent, older brother or sister, etc.

- Are you doing anything to avoid this transference from the child to the teacher? Are you doing anything to avoid being treated as if you are their parent, older brother or sister? If not, can you put something into place?

- Focus on the system and organisation – are there any aspects of organisation within school that either support or hinder this child's emotional, social and behaviour development? Where does the child experience success? Are there any areas within the curriculum where the child experiences success? Do you have a pastoral system within school? Is it effectively accessed by the child?

- Use this moment in time to allow the person recording all of the key points to summarise the content and bring the attention of the group to any emerging themes so far.

- From the picture so far, can you pull out any understanding, thoughts or hypotheses? This is an important part of the process, as it is key to keep thinking in depth and as open-endedly as possible. You need to invite as many possible hypotheses as you can. The members of the group need to be led through this mind map of understanding and possible theories that may be used to explain what is happening in this situation.

- What alternative strategies and different interventions could be used? Mind map as many alternatives as you can in the group and record them. As a shared session, all participants are expected to contribute, including the person presenting the situations. You just need to make sure that you are not overloaded with strategies. The person presenting has the final say on what strategy you will be selecting and moving forward with.

- Agree the first steps that you will take. The person presenting the issue selects the next steps that will be taken and the strategies that they will be using. Appoint a 'coach', who will check in with that person. Agree deadlines for the completion of the first steps. The 'coach' can check that the deadlines have been met.

- The final step of the session that needs to be taken is to get everybody to stand, form a circle and reflect on the process.

Behaviour scripts and social stories

These are two very separate strategies. We will look at both of these and support you with introducing them into your setting.

Social stories

Social stories may be something that you have used before, with children with ASD, but I don't see many people using them with children who exhibit social, emotional and mental health difficulties. They are a fantastic tool to introduce, and they're free!

Social expectations when interacting with others are typically learned through role-modelling. Children with SEMH difficulties sometimes need more explicit instructions. Social stories are meant to help children understand social situations, expectations, social cues, new activities and/or social rules. They are brief descriptive stories providing accurate information regarding a social situation. Children are more likely to act within social expectations when situations are modelled for them. You can use these simple stories as a tool to prepare the child for a new situation, to address problem behaviour, or even to teach new skills.

There is a set of rules that you need to follow to ensure that the social story will actually be effective with the child. Firstly, try to write the story with the child's perspective in mind. If your child is old enough, then ideally you'd like to try to write the story together.

There are three types of sentence used in writing social stories:

1. Descriptive sentences: these objectively define events – where the situation occurs, who is involved, what they are doing and why (e.g. when children are working, they sit down in their chairs).

2. Perspective sentences: these describe the internal status of the person or persons involved – their thoughts, feelings or moods (e.g. running inside could hurt me or other people).

3. Directive sentences: these are desired responses stated in a positive manner. They may begin with 'I can try…' or 'I will work on…' (e.g. I will try to sit in my seat). Try to avoid sentences starting with 'do not' or definitive statements.

A social story should have three to five descriptive and perspective sentences for each directive sentence. Avoid using too many directive sentences; they may make the story too negative.

Finally, include age-appropriate pictures in the social story. If you can include a picture of your child, then even better.

Here is an example of a social story that works within these rules and which you could use in your setting:

Running out of the classroom

I like to run out of my classroom.
It makes me feel happy to escape.
It's okay to run when I am playing outside.
I can run when I am on the playground at breaktime and lunchtime.

Sometimes I feel like running out of the classroom but it is safer to stay with my teacher.

Running out of the classroom could hurt me or upset my teacher.

When children are in class they don't run out of the classroom.

I will try to stay in my classroom and only run when I am outside on the playground.

My teachers and parents like it when I stay in my classroom.

Make sure that you have a go and write your own. Share them with others. The more we share, the bigger our network and the more access we have to resources that will support ALL of our children.

Behaviour scripts

Behaviour scripts can be used at a time of crisis for a child. During Chapter 4 on extreme behaviours, we mentioned that when a child is at their crisis point, they are in a heightened state with adrenaline pumping. At this point, they are not often able to listen to what you are saying, so the calmness of a behaviour script is welcome.

You may already be familiar with behaviour scripts but for those of you that aren't, a behaviour script is a clear set of statements that all members of staff use when they are dealing with a child in crisis.

One behaviour script does not need to follow the same rules as another but does need to be simple and clear so that the child is more likely to be able to hear it. A way in which you can set it up is to ask the adults working with the child to get together and basically ask what works — for example, time to reflect/cool down or choices. Also ask for triggers that you'll need to avoid when a child is heightened before writing the behaviour script.

Here is an example of a behaviour script if your child is struggling with their anger and is at crisis point in their behaviours:

1. Identify/label the problem, e.g. 'I can see that you're angry'.

2. State the reason, e.g. 'You're angry because you feel that you haven't been listened to'.

3. Offer a strategy, e.g. 'I'm here to help you'/'When I am angry I count down from five'/'Come and sit down and explain what has happened'.

4. Give general reassurance, e.g. 'Keep talking and I'll always listen'.

The behaviour script needs to be consistently used by all adults involved with the child. You must not make any additions to it when you are dealing with the child as they need the consistency during these times of crisis. The consistency will act as their boundaries. Once you have calmed down the situation using your script, then you are able to use the conflict resolution to deal with any incidents that have arisen or use your instructions within the child's behaviour plan for these next steps.

You may want to create cards for all staff involved with your children, copy the behaviour script onto it and get the staff to wear it on their lanyard to enable them all to be consistent in their resolution of crisis behaviours. As with other strategies and interventions, if it isn't consistent, then it will not support a child and ultimately enable them to learn how to deal with their emotions and behaviours.

Questioning to support children

That question of knowing what to say during daily life is a difficult one. As humans, we fill silence. Sometimes we speak before we think. This can be overloading for a child who needs their focus to be on their behaviour, rather than having to focus on unnecessary parts of speech.

Think about a situation where your child has had an incident. You're in the middle of a heated crisis, you are usually dealing with two separate people and their emotions, and you've normally got a time restraint and a growing crowd. You feel pressure to get to the bottom of the issue, deal with each child in the way that you need to and carry on with your teaching/break duty, and so on.

It's at this point that we may descend into a monologue of…

'But how many times have I told you that you shouldn't be playing with Alex? It never ends well and I wish that you'd listen to me! What should you have done? Why didn't you do it? We've put so much effort into thinking through all those different strategies and you didn't use one! Now tell me what happened!'

Don't pretend you're not smiling. When we invest so much in some-body, we let ourselves believe that an issue can be solved quickly. It's an ongoing investment and there will be bumps in the road. We're dealing with children while sometimes expecting them to learn in an adult way. External factors can easily cloud your judgment and fudge your reaction. And, knowing your luck, Alex's mum could be a tricky parent and you have the added pressure of knowing that, regardless of the incident or whether there was blame, you're going to have to explain the situation.

At the point of beginning to deal with the incident, you are able to use restorative practice and conflict resolution to deal with the incident but, on a daily basis of supporting your child, you need to change your use of language.

If your child does something inappropriate then, rather than asking your child to explain their inappropriate behaviour, you need to be dir-ective, calm and just state your expectations. This doesn't just apply to children who find it hard to manage their behaviour; this applies to the way in which you interact with all children.

I'm providing you with some examples of questions that you may typically ask within a classroom situation, and which you do need to begin to try to avoid. Each question follows with a more proactive response to behaviour, and one that is more likely to receive a positive response in return.

- You may as well just avoid questions where you don't want the answer to be one that you don't want to hear, such as **'Are you going into assembly now?'**

Assemblies can be one of those hot spots – everybody sitting all together in a stuffy room. You have to be silent while you listen to at least 30 minutes of the same person talking over and over again, while there are people in front of you, behind you and next to you that are just itching to get prodded and poked by you. Then there's the music – you go from endless monologue to exciting music that you love, so it's even more fun to throw your arms around and dance in an uncontrollable manner. As a teacher, you may want to think about having assemblies as a time for intervention but, if this is not possible, then be directive: **'It is time to go into assembly.'**

- Also avoid questions that may escalate into refusal, such as **'Why don't you just finish your work?'**

  If children are bubbling and coming off task or hanging around rather than going outside, then they could be seeking support from themselves or you, and are at that stage where their behaviour can still be channelled. Instead of this directive question, provide a statement that will show children what is coming next, such as **'Once you have completed reading your book, then it is fruit time.'**

- Avoid asking a question if it provides no answer, such as **'How many times have I asked you to put your pencil away?'**

  It's at this point where you're bubbling yourself. One option would be just to quietly signal another member of staff to swap in whilst you have a second to calm down. The other would be simply to just mentally take a step back, breathe and give the alternative responses of ignoring the fact that they haven't put their pencil away, waiting until they've done it and then providing a positive comment, or giving them an option similar to the one above so that they know their choices, such as **'Put your pencil in the pot and then it's time for break.'**

- Don't ask questions that you know would prompt a child to feel that lying is the only way out, such as **'Did you steal Jamie's crisps from his lunchbox?'**

  Firstly, you need to eliminate the possibility that your child is stealing for need, and ensure that they have enough food for themselves to eat. This may seem like a strange thing for you to read but, unfortunately, there are children who aren't being fed and feel that they have no alternative but to take other people's food. Once you've eliminated this, then say nothing until you have proof, and then deal with the situation as you would do any other incident.

- Avoid questions where the child's answer is obvious. If you've seen your child draw all over somebody else's work, then don't say **'Did you just draw on Joe's work?'**

  There's no point in asking this question when you know that they did. Prompt them to correct what they have done wrong – for example,

'Get a rubber to help Joe repair his work. Thank you' or **'Get a new piece of paper for Joe.'**

This issue will need dealing with at a later time but your first priority is to support Joe, who will be either worried that his work has been ruined and he doesn't have time to correct it or upset that his work has been destroyed by someone else. You will also have noticed that I modelled the use of the words 'thank you'. This isn't because I am fantastic with my manners, although I am. Nor does it mean I am condoning what the child has done. I use it because it doesn't imply choice. It is directive. If I said **'Get a rubber to help Joe repair his work, please?'** then there is the option of a 'no'. In my response, there is no such option.

Use these ideas to support you in developing genuine relationships with your children and, in turn, you will be able to support them in minimising their disruptive behaviour. You invest in them and slowly they will invest in you. It will give them a reason to behave, and modifying behaviour will become more attainable.

Chapter 9
Assessment

I'm sure that you will all have flicked to this chapter because finding information on how to assess SEMH children is as rare as finding a leprechaun at the end of a rainbow. Well, here's the end of the rainbow and I'm your leprechaun. We're going to be discussing different types of assessments that you'll be able to take into your classroom and use as forms of assessment for SEMH children.

Strengths and Difficulties Questionnaire

The Strengths and Difficulties Questionnaire (SDQ) is a brief behavioural screening questionnaire for children from the age of three to 16 years old. The SDQ questions you about 25 attributes belonging to the child that you are filling it out for. These attributes are both positive and negative. They are divided into five different areas: emotional, conduct, hyperactivity, relationships that they have with their peers and prosocial behaviour. The SDQ includes questions for children and young people, parents and staff. When using all of these options, you are able to create a group profile of the child concerned. If you haven't used this questionnaire before, then there are two different options. You can fill out a paper copy or there is a link to the online version in the 'Further reading' section.

There are many positives in using the SDQ to inform you more about your child:

- It can be used before you plan and deliver your block of intervention.

- You can use it to enable you to pinpoint specific difficulties and then use this to target your intervention more effectively.

- You are able to create a fuller profile, as it's not just your views that are taken into account to form it; there are also those from other staff and parents, as well as the child.

- It highlights the area of difficulty and allows you to make comparisons – for example, at school compared to at home. You are able to use this information to help you to identify strategies that will enable you to support the child's development and behaviour in both settings.

- Make sure if you are seeking further support from outside agencies that you give them copies of your various SDQs. Also provide these for parents if they are seeking their own support.

Case study: Joanna – aged ten

Joanna doesn't stand out in your class. She has a few friends and doesn't get involved with any friendship issues that you have been having to deal with lately. She is average in terms of academic ability and does reach age-related expectations (ARE) across all subjects. When you think of difficulties in behaviour, you wouldn't think of Joanna, but there is something that you can't identify. You're not quite sure whether she is fully engaged with her friendships or whether she plays superficially alongside others. You don't feel that it warrants a discussion with your SENDCo or even with her parents, whom you don't see very often now that she's ten.

You wouldn't think that a child like Joanna would feature in this book but the reason that she does is that behaviour isn't always visible. It is your job to support all of the children in your class and enable all of them to achieve their individual potential. On the surface of it, Joanna may get overlooked as she's achieving ARE in all areas, but there are a few indicators that imply that she isn't engaging fully. This should excite you, as there is more that you can do in your learning journey with Joanna.

What can I do to move forward with Joanna?

- Include her as a good role model for a social skills group. Although she isn't demonstrating behaviour that would make me action a social skills group specifically for her, she would benefit from the skill set provided within it. Include one of her friends so that you can observe these friendships too.

- Complete an SDQ with Joanna in mind. It will help you to see whether there is anything further that you can identify, and consequently you can put support into place for her.

- Set her little challenges. Is she really an ARE child or could she be pushed?

- Monitor her behaviour and interactions over time.

Customised assessments

Now, assessments don't always need to be assessments that others have designed. If you think about the term, simply by definition you are using a tool to help you to find out more about your child in your chosen area. You may want to use simple assessments looking at a child and compare them over time. For example:

1	There is no problem that I cannot solve when I try hard enough.
2	I am able to get what I want when I explain myself.
3	It is easy for me to stick to the rules and achieve what I want.
4	I am confident when I am in new situations.
5	If something changes, I can be flexible.
6	I can work well with any child.
7	I cope well under pressure.
8	I am able to find several solutions when there is a problem in front of me.
9	If I am in trouble, I know what to do to help myself.
10	I am not easily fazed.

Give your children a scale to work to in order for them to assess themselves. One like this would work:

1	2	3	4
Agree			Disagree

Of course, you can change your questions to whatever you need to focus on, but you could use an assessment similar to this in a variety of ways:

- Use it over time to see how things change. It will allow you to see any movement, improvement or decline over the year.

- Use it to assign roles – for example, if you were doing a group work intervention, then you could use questions relating to self-esteem. You may want to put the child who scores the lowest on self-esteem questions in charge of your group game so that you can facilitate them and support them in their development.

- Use it as a way of communicating progress with parents.

- Children could assess themselves. You could assess them and you could compare the results together.

Case study: Tomek – aged eleven

Tomek is a quiet member of your class. He engages in lessons and has good friendships. He enjoys games on the playground and always follows the rules. The work that he produces is always to a high standard and he always produces work when working in a group. His mum and dad are supportive of Tomek and you do see them taking an active role in Tomek's school life and sporting achievements. Tomek has never had a cause for concern so there have not been any discussions with the SENDCo nor any issues raised with Tomek's parents.

How can you use these assessments to support Tomek?

Like Joanna, Tomek could easily be overlooked, and an assessment like this is perfect to identify Tomek's points for improvement. Although he has solid friendships and is engaging on the playground and in lessons, Tomek is quieter. An assessment like this would enable you to identify where best to support Tomek. If using this assessment with a group, then it may turn out that Tomek is shyer than the other members of the group and may prompt you to have Tomek as a group leader.

Well-being scales

Scales can be adapted for so much and give you room for measuring improvement and decline. A scale isn't going to provide completely accurate data, as it raises questions over what 7/10 actually means and how you measure it, but it does provide soft data where sometimes there is no other data. I like to use scales as you can have a discussion with the children about what each number denotes. For younger children, you can discuss a scale and link it to a ladder.

When discussing well-being with the children and putting as much effort into well-being as we discussed in Chapter 6, it is useful to monitor this and then assess it. Scales/ladders are a perfect way to do this.

Start by asking a simple question to the child that you are working with:

How happy are you with your whole life at the moment?

Then introduce questions to enable you to gather information on the children's well-being. If you conduct this on a termly basis then, again, it gives you some comparable data.

Examples of statements for children to rate using this scale are:

I can't do anything right	
In general, I like being the way that I am	
I do a lot of important things	
Overall I have a lot to be proud of	
I can do things as well as most other people	
Overall I am good	
Other people think I am a good person	
I am as good as most other people	
When I do something I do it well	

Introduce the following set of statements but be clear with the children that they are rating these based on themselves:

I cry a lot	
I am too fearful or anxious	
I am nervous or tense	
I am unhappy, sad or depressed	
I worry a lot	

These questions may bring about deep discussions with your child, so make sure that you've set aside extra time in case they need that time to go into detail about their thoughts and feelings.

Continue with the next set of statements and, again, be clear with your child that they are rating these based on themselves:

I usually manage one way or another	
I keep interested in things	
I feel that my life has a sense of purpose	
I find life really worth living	
My life has meaning	

Again, there are some tricky topics within this so just be mindful of the issues with timing, as above, but also think about where it is that you're filling this out. Ideally, a quiet and private space is perfect.

Introduce the next set of statements but make sure that the children know they are rating the following about themselves and their friends:

My friends treat me well	
I have a lot of fun with my friends	
My friends are mean to me	
My friends are great	
My friends will help me if I need it	

The next set of statements needs to be rated with regard to the children and their families:

I enjoy being at home with my family	
I like spending time with my parents	
My parents and I do fun things together	
My parents treat me fairly	
My family gets along well together	
I get help with my homework if I need it	
I find it easy to get to sleep at night	

The following statements need to be thought about in relation to your child and where they live:

I play out in my neighbourhood	
I wish that I lived somewhere else	
I like where I live	
There are lots of fun things to do where I live	
I wish there were different people in my neighbourhood	

The statements then start moving on to the child thinking about their opinions, thoughts and feelings about school:

I like being in school	
I wish that I didn't have to go to school	
I feel safe at school	
I enjoy school activities	
School is interesting	
My teachers listen to my opinions	
I learn about everything that I'd like to	
I know who to go to if I am upset, worried or need to talk	

I feel that I am well challenged with my work at school	
It is important to come to school every day	
There isn't any bullying at my school	
My worries are always sorted out by people at school	

Case study: Johnny – aged nine

Johnny is a lively child. He has been in your school since Early Years Foundation Stage (EYFS). Johnny had an unstable family life from four to nine years old. You've provided support for his parents through parents' support services and have always had a good relationship with his parents. Since Johnny turned nine, you have seen an improvement in their stability. This has had a positive impact on Johnny. You have been working hard with Johnny on his behaviour since he started at your school. During the first few years, he demonstrated particularly difficult behaviours, which you and your team supported him in changing. Since then, he has been able to work on his academic progress and now has been able to make huge strides in improving both his behaviour and academic attainment. Johnny works weekly with a Pastoral Support Worker and this has been crucial to his success.

How can you use the well-being scales to support Johnny?

You've seen the progress that Johnny has made and the huge benefit the relationship with his Pastoral Support Worker has had. Linking all of his supports, including school and home, has enabled Johnny to have that support around him. The big issue screaming out is that of transition. Johnny is nearly 10 years old and will be losing the biggest support that he has had during his school life. You can use the well-being scale during his final year so that he can see his shift into independence. Using this scale and the different statements, you will help Johnny to compartmentalise the different areas of support as well as identify weaker areas and help him to think of support strategies for the future. The issue of transition is one of great worry for children who have difficulty with their behaviour. We must build the area of independence for them or else they will risk losing all of the progress that they have made during their primary school years.

Boxall Profile and nurture groups

The Boxall Profile provides you with a precise assessment of children who appear to be struggling with a variety of different areas. It will help you to be specific when planning your intervention with those children who you may come across whose behaviour seems so difficult that you don't know where to start! It provides you with a breakdown of their behaviour, enables you to look beyond the behaviour and gives you a starting point, as well as leading you comfortably into progress. It's also extremely useful to share with your classroom staff.

Although it is not a free assessment (unlike the SDQ), it is very easy to use and comes with clear guidelines for you to complete it. It is completed in two parts and must be completed by the staff who know the children the best within your classroom setting. As I mentioned earlier, the fact that it is so constructive is of huge benefit because, as soon as it's completed, you can plan your specific interventions straight away. I'd also recommend that you complete it on a half-termly/eight-weekly basis so that you can check and celebrate progress and always stay focused on the most difficult strands for the child.

The profile was first developed as part of the nurture group movement, which began in 1969. Nurture groups were developed by Marjorie Boxall, who was an educational psychologist. There was great social upheaval and huge levels of teacher shortages at the time, and this was a response to the high levels of distress experienced by primary schools. Special schools had seen a huge rise in referrals from schools that were referring children who would be classed as having social, emotional and mental health difficulties. This became unmanageable and schools had high turnover rates: 50% turnover was not uncommon.

Boxall implemented a new and alternative way of focusing more deeply on the behaviour that was limiting the academic progress of children in schools. I feel strongly that we cannot expect great academic progress until we support children in progressing with their behaviour.

Boxall focused on the early development of children, the attitudes that had been projected onto them and what they projected at school (self-concept).

She identified the difficulties presented and highlighted the links between these difficulties and the impoverished early nurturing that the children had experienced. She felt that, by lacking adequate experience of being and feeling cherished and attended to, for whatever reason, children were unable to form, make and respond appropriately to the other children and adults that they encountered in their daily life. Therefore, the children were wholly unprepared and not ready for the demands of school life. They were unable to meet the social and intellectual demands of life in school and so were set up, without intervention, to fail at school.

At this time, teachers were focused on 'child-centred' education but also knew that, in order for this to be successful, children needed to be able to organise themselves, sit around a table and cooperate with different children, with less structure and supervision than they were previously used to.

As soon as nurture groups were established in inner London, great progress was achieved with children who had previously been on the verge of internal, temporary or permanent exclusions. Staff were able to see this progress, which reaffirmed these groups in schools. Hand in hand with this improvement came a great improvement in staff morale, as all staff and assistants saw that they were able to improve a child's life by facilitating them in developing the skills that they needed to succeed.

A nurture group usually has two staff: normally a teacher and an assistant. They understand the developmental processes of childhood. They also understand and accept that some children can get stuck at an early stage of this process and need experiences appropriate to the stage in which they are stuck in order to support them to move on.

Trust is the first thing that children need during this process. The staff within the nurture groups must know this. It is achieved by demonstrating unfaltering acceptance of the child as they are. As the child's confidence grows, then the staff need to offer work appropriate to the stage that they have reached. They need to implement secure routines that are always explained. Staff must not assume that there is any prior knowledge of any routine or boundary implemented in the setting.

There are six clear principles of a nurture group:

1. Children's learning is understood developmentally.
2. The classroom offers a safe base.
3. The importance of nurture for the development of well-being.
4. Language is a vital means of communication.
5. ALL behaviour is communication.
6. The importance of transition in children's lives.

In addition to the above principles, within this setting the child is always listened to. Staff are expected to do what every attentive parent does: commenting on what the child tells them, expanding it and putting it into a wider context. This enables the child to make sense of their world. Within the nurture group, it is not just skills that are taught. Academic content is taught but it must be in a way that fits in with the child's individual developmental needs. Again, this is repeating the fact that academic progress will not be sustainable or see appropriate improvement and progress unless children are ready developmentally.

Boxall was active in sharing her knowledge of child development. She was central to the nurture group movement. Her role was active and she worked extensively with staff who worked in nurture groups. She trained staff to look at the maladaptive behaviour that they were often presented with and changed their thinking, enabling them to look deeper at the underlying distress they were experiencing.

As the nurture group movement grew and more progress was seen, those involved did what we are doing in this chapter: looked for a form of assessment, measuring the change that they were seeing and the progress that the children were making. This was the very beginning of the Boxall Profile.

The experiences that nurture groups have had in the past have instilled a greater understanding of the emotional content of learning, which you will now have experienced as 'emotional literacy'. We know how this should not be limited to only children that struggle with their own social, emotional and mental health difficulties, but that it is absolutely vital to ALL children. This nurture group mentality can help you to implement a positive language that needs to be embedded. Unfortunately, children in school can be insecure about their worth and unable to articulate their feelings appropriately, all as a result of 'being stuck' in a stage of development. As a result, you can be presented with very confused behaviours, including withdrawal when the children are showing their discomfort in social situations, while watching children achieve much less than their potential and struggling to form any worthwhile relationships. You can also be presented with children acting out their feelings of failure and anger (at themselves and/or others) through minor and major acts of disruption to school and the progress of others. As a teacher, one of the hardest things to see is a child who does not become positively engaged in their education and all of the opportunities that having a good education presents. By understanding the reasons for behaviour, we can move forward and support children more effectively.

How to use the Boxall Profile

The profile has two sections. Each section consists of a list of 34 descriptive items that, as I mentioned previously, must be completed by someone who knows the child well within the classroom.

The two sections relate to developmental strands and the diagnostic profile.

Section I: Developmental strands

This measures a child's progress through the different aspects of development during their pre-school years. In order for a child to be able to make good and effective use of the opportunities presented to them during their education, they need to be able to complete their first stage of learning. Realistically, the child that you will be completing your Boxall assessment on will have missed out on some of these developmental stages so, by being able to identify both the child's strengths and weaknesses within this assessment, staff are able to focus on the areas that the child struggles with the most and provide the extra support that they need. Within this section, there are two clusters. The first assesses the child's organisation of their learning experiences and the second assesses their internalisation of controls. Within each cluster, there are five columns.

Section II: The diagnostic profile

This section consists of descriptive items that describe the behaviours that act as inhibitors or interfere with the child's satisfactory and appropriate involvement with school and in school life. They can be either directly or indirectly the outcome of any impaired learning during the child's earliest years. This section of the profile has three clusters: self-limiting features, undeveloped behaviour and unsupported development.

Using the profile

The scores that are achieved on the developmental strands are important. Think of them as the building blocks in a child's development. If the foundations are missing, then we need to fill those foundations. We can do this by providing experiences for the children to have and enabling them to make sense of these experiences. This section shows you what progress has been made so far with the child and pinpoints where the help is needed the most. The diagnostic profile gets you to start looking at the child with a fresh perspective.

What do the scores suggest?

When 'self-limiting' features are highlighted, this implies that there is something preventing the child from engagement with the world. To be able to support children who have these features as predominant, staff would need to provide a warm and supportive relationship, which could prove to be quite difficult. In order to be able to achieve this, staff will need to be confident in their ability to do so, and this would also take a lot of time and patience, particularly when hurdles appear.

If a child scores highly in the area of 'undeveloped behaviour', then it suggests that a child has not developed the inner skills and resources that are required to adjust to life at school, due to having minimal help during their early stages of life. The child may present as demanding, disorganised and immature in comparison to expectations and their peers. This is incredibly difficult for school staff. The responses that the child may get will reduce their self-confidence, and behaviours will escalate. We all know that staff can find it extremely difficult to look beyond the behaviours of a child to the underlying causes, and may even feel that excuses are being made. By having these scores to refer to, staff will be able to see the underlying causes of the behaviour. Attitudes in staff do change and they are then able to start planning in order to meet the child's needs. Consequently, there is an impact on the child's maturity level. Although the child will continue functioning within the early stages, they will now have the potential for attachment and, therefore, will be likely to respond well to an early-level relationship and other experiences appropriate for them.

A worrying outcome would be high scores in the 'unsupported development' strands. This would be highly undesirable as it suggests that there was a profound lack of nurturing care in the child's early life. It could even signpost abusive behaviour. The child protects themselves from hurt and total loss of self-regard through behaviours and difficulties that staff may have trouble in managing, and there is the potential for mental illness and criminality presenting later on in life. These early experiences all result in children having had no reason to trust the adults within their world. The earlier that we are able to identify children who sit within this category, the greater chance that we have of being able to support them and their behaviour and, in turn, change their attitudes, giving them a greater chance of having a more successful and productive life. If a child is scoring heavily in the earlier columns, then it tells us they are directing their hurt more inwardly. They can be helped and supported by staff who are not only able to understand the origins of their behaviour but can also offer patient and supportive teaching. However, if the underlying behaviour is scoring higher in the later columns, then this behaviour is directed at others. The behaviour is more likely to lead to internalised and organised anti-social behaviour patterns, which bring a sense of satisfaction to a child. It is going to take early and more skilled intervention, as these behaviours are more difficult to change.

What can I do with my results?

You need to have an in-depth look at what the diagnostic profile is showing you and reflect on this. You could even complete the 'circle of adults' intervention that was detailed in the previous chapter with this in mind. The problem-solving sequence that forms a part of this can be used to come up with strategies that you could implement and use to support the child. Some developmental strands are much easier to interpret – e.g. participates constructively – and you will find it easier to be able to implement an intervention that you can make progress with. With the strands that present more difficult behaviours, deeper thought and reflection are needed on how to move forward with these.

Case study: Max – aged seven

Max's behaviour is unpredictable and, at times, uncontrollable. You feel that you have a good relationship with Max but there is no way of being able to see when these behaviours will arise. You are completing your ABC charts to pinpoint any patterns and have written a behaviour plan, but you are struggling to be specific in your targets, as all areas seem to be a problem. The behaviours are affecting other people in your class as well as Max himself. He has failed to meet age-related expectations and can often refuse to work, even when it is something that you think he may enjoy. Although he appears to enjoy sport, Max looks as though he cannot cooperate with anybody in a team game, and when he perceives an injustice he can often lash out. You struggle to see Max's likes and, when you probe, Max replies that he doesn't like anything and everything is stupid. Max does have a sense of humour. You find it frustrating that you feel you cannot find a way to support Max. Max lives at home with his grandma. He does see his mum and dad separately but it is sporadic. You have made referrals to Family Support but the family does not engage.

You know when you have a child like Max in your class. Your colleagues do nothing but comment negatively on everything that he does, and they are constantly asking why he is allowed to 'get away' with it. If you try to probe the attitudes of your colleagues further, then 'getting away' with it constitutes a lack of exclusion for his behaviour. You know that you need to be that positive force in Max's life and encourage other staff to do the same, but you don't know where to start in supporting Max. With no perceived rewards, you don't know how to provide a worthwhile intervention to implement and it's a real 'head in hands' moment.

The Boxall Profile would provide you with a real sense of support here. It may even be useful to complete one yourself and ask a member of staff whose negative attitudes are apparent to complete one for your own comparison. Reflect in the outcomes together. Show them that Max's behaviour comes from an underlying difficulty and/or reason. Start this journey of support for Max together so that you can see real change. When there appear to be so many difficulties and high priorities, the Boxall Profile allows you to find out the one that he finds most hard. Start there. Provide that nurture group environment using the principles discussed earlier. It's not too late for Max. Year 3 is halfway through his primary education, and there is time to be able to support Max to realise success within his life and a real sense of worth within your school community. Staff will see change and they will support in time.

When the times come to discuss data with your head teacher, you sometimes see a lack of progression in academics with those children who demonstrate difficult behaviour. Make sure that you highlight alternative progression so that you can show how effective you are being. These assessments will help you to do that.

Chapter 10
CPD

Behaviour is so contentious that sometimes we struggle to feel in control. There's even contention over semantics – behaviour, SEMH… When we're talking about children and wanting to support children, we shouldn't have to worry about terminology. It is different with changes in the curriculum. We are provided with the change, CPD can be offered and our subject knowledge grows. It is not often that there is a proactive approach to behaviour and that there is constant growth in subject knowledge within a mainstream primary setting. Normally it's the case that we zoom around within our daily life, fitting as much as we can into the hours that we teach, supporting our children, and a child exhibiting SEMH can then send our heads spinning.

If our children have a diagnosed condition, such as ADHD, then there is a range of CPD support available, but you know as well as I do that it cannot be individual unless you are working on a one-to-one basis with a specialist. And if you have more than one child with a diagnosed condition, then that will bring more challenges for you to overcome. Generally, if you are looking for CPD that enables you to deepen your knowledge and understanding of behaviour and the underlying reasons for it, then I will talk you through ways of doing this continuously without big price tags attached.

Firstly, you've made a great choice in reading this book – an excellent form of CPD!

Networking

Networking is free. By acquiring key contacts that have different experiences of behaviour in schools, you gain people that you can have formal and informal discussions with. Your contacts don't need to be people that have qualifications or are consultants in behaviour – although, if you can find these contacts, keep them! Your contacts can be and should be people that have been in similar situations: LSAs that have experienced a whole host of different behaviour strategies or other teachers that have encountered problems. Build these connections and you will be able to utilise them, gain strategies for your own personal toolkit and then disseminate them to others.

It is absolutely free to call your local schools. Some special schools and PRUs have an outreach service (some free and some not) that will be able to support you within school with strategies for different children. They may also be able to provide you with ideas on how you can instil confidence and a positive attitude in your colleagues. Staff in special schools and PRUs will experience the difficulties that you face on a more regular basis, so one of the many benefits of liaising with these members of staff is that they will be able to provide you with a clear and detached view of the difficulties that you may be facing. A fresh perspective on a difficult situation is like gold dust. Utilise these links where possible and don't forget that networking is two-way. You will have a lot to offer back to staff from these schools as well. You may have fresh ideas and new interventions that you will be able to talk to them about too.

Talk to your local PRU about any panels that they offer. Some offer a panel where you can take a case study along in order to discuss all of the information, including the child in your setting, what behaviours they present on a typical day and any other behaviours that they present, so that the members of staff can have a full picture of the child. The staff members from the PRU then usually discuss the child, along with any strategies that may be useful, and systems and processes that you can put in place to try to support your child in school. It is also good when other people within the panel have a chance to support you too and think of any strategies that they have used in similar cases. The two-way process is again paramount, as you are able to offer your ideas with other cases as well. If you are able to send more than one member of staff, it is good for self-esteem, works as a confidence booster and provides empowerment for staff.

You will have noticed that I have used the words 'usually' and 'some' because not all specialist provision offers this service. However, you don't need to wait for them to start. There will be a wealth of experience in your own setting, within your family of schools, local authorities and/

or academy trusts. Send out information and start your own group to discuss individual cases. There is nothing to stop you from benefiting from each other's expertise and pulling out ideas that may be applicable to you. Don't forget the golden rule of confidentiality. As we have said previously, behaviour is contentious and discussing behaviour can cause upset. Remove the name and depersonalise the case.

Coaching

We use coaching for upskilling in academic subjects and deepening subject knowledge, so why not use it for behaviour? Have a look at your colleagues and link people up. Organise time for them to go and watch each other, with a sole focus on behaviour. Be clear with them that nobody is watching each other; they are simply catching ideas to support their behaviour management. Use your opportunities to grab as many strategies as you can, write them down and reflect. Once you have completed all of your coaching sessions, get together for a staff meeting. Share all of the positives that you have seen so that you can gain as many ideas as possible and grasp all of the positive methods that are happening within your school.

Video conferencing

Widen your network even further by exploring the option of doing it online. Set up your own video conferencing and have a discussion with each other. There are free apps and websites that will enable you to access video conferencing with ease, and there are free YouTube videos that can talk you through how to set it up. If all else fails, network with your ICT technician, who will be able to set this up for you.

Positives of video conferencing

- You can network with different colleagues all over the world.
- It eliminates the difficulty of arranging a time and place for all colleagues to travel and physically meet with each other.

- All that you need to agree on is a time to meet.
- Due to its flexibility, you can meet as often as your schedule allows.

Negatives of video conferencing

- You have to rely on an internet connection.
- Technology can sometimes fail.
- You need somebody to agree to chair the session so that all people can have a turn in speaking and everybody gets the same out of the meeting.

Blogging

In terms of self-reflection, this is an incredible tool.

Tips for blogging

- Set up a space for your blog. I use Blogger (www.behaviourteach. blogspot.co.uk) – it's quite simple to use. You do need a Gmail account, but it is a good space for the relaxed blogger. If you are wanting to blog regularly and have different pages, then you may want to consider the alternative platforms.
- Read other people's blogs, which don't necessarily have to be on behaviour. Here are some that I read regularly (the web addresses can be found in the 'Further reading' section):
  - Special needs teaching and education (@JW_Teach) – written by Joe White, an assistant head teacher who blogs about SEND and behaviour.
  - SENexchangeuk – led by Cherryl Drabble and Mary Isherwood, who blog specifically about SEND.
  - Teacher toolkit – written by Ross Morrison McGill, who blogs on a variety of different topics in education. He is also known as @TeacherToolkit!
  - Inclusion – Mark Allen blogs on behaviour. Full of super articles and extremely interesting.

- Jordyjax – Jackie Ward is an ex-deputy head in a PRU, who is now on the journey to becoming a consultant. She regularly updates her blogs and always chooses excellent topics to talk about.

- Write your first post for yourself. Don't worry about your audience – just get it out there.

- Don't worry about what you are writing. Someone somewhere will connect with it. Your readership may not be huge, so write for yourself.

- Don't panic about how you sound. I honestly think that your personality comes through in your writing. When I read somebody's blog, I feel like I am hearing them in conversation, listening to their innermost thoughts and feelings.

- Feel like you are empowered. I look back now at my initial blogs and think 'Oh my goodness, did I really write that?' Behaviour is ever-changing. Things I wrote about three years ago may have changed. Things that I thought three years ago may have been revised by new experiences and/or exposure to new CPD or concepts. That's okay! It's nice to see how behaviour has changed and look at how your journey in blogging has developed.

- Publish your blogs. Go on! Hit that button and make sure that you tag me in (@behaviourteach), so that I can read it and share it with my followers too!

Social media

Twitter and Facebook are both amazing ways of interacting with a variety of different people on the topic of behaviour, as well as using them for your own CPD. I cannot praise social media highly enough. There are a variety of different chats that you can get involved with.

How to get involved with a Twitter chat

1. Log in to your Twitter account.
2. Search for your chosen chat in the 'search' bar.
3. Click 'All Tweets'.

4. Reply to those you want to engage with.

5. Don't forget to include your hashtag so that others can see your comments and connect with you

Twitter chats that you must engage with

1. #behaviourchat

Not just because I host it! Behaviour Chat has been established for over three years now. We have different weekly hosts and are always looking for new people to host, so make sure that as soon as you are a seasoned Tweeter, you offer to do it. It will be great CPD and a great experience. People on Twitter come up with questions, and we get together and discuss them. We have a variety of different participants, including teachers, support staff, SLT, consultants, etc.

#behaviourchat runs during term time on a Monday and is on from 8.00–8.30/ 9.00pm (dependent on host).

2. #SENexchange

This is led by the same hosts as the blog: Mary Isherwood and Cherryl Drabble, who are both very knowledgeable in the area of SEND. Again, there are a variety of participants and the topics are extremely specific, so you can really discuss issues that you may be facing in your classroom. *#SENexchange runs on a Wednesday and is on from 8.00–8.30pm. There is always a 'storify' for you to look at in case you miss the chat itself.*

3. #primaryrocks

This chat was set up by Graham Andre and Rob Smith to promote primary schools. It is focused on education chat specific to primary schools. A variety of different participants ask questions prior to the chat and four questions are chosen to be discussed during the hour. *#primaryrocks runs every Monday, including non-term time, and is on from 8.00–9.00pm.*

4. #SLTchat

This is led by different hosts each week and focuses on different whole-school questions. It is an education chat that is not specific to either primary or secondary, but is wholly focused on issues that affect the whole school. The education minister and DfE have been past hosts. Even if you don't feel confident to join in with this one, make sure that you become an enthusiastic lurker!

#SLTchat runs every Sunday during term time and is on from 8.00–8.30pm.

5. #NQTchat

This is a weekly chat for teachers just entering the profession. There are also experienced teachers that join in as well. Behaviour does feature within these chats, so you may want to dip in and out to find out the different strategies that others have.

#NQTchat runs every Wednesday from 8.00–9.00pm.

6. #ittchat

This is led by three people, @EdTeachFocused, @MartinGSaunders and @TrainingToTeach, and is aimed at those who are just entering the profession. All of those burning questions are answered for people just starting on their journey. If this is you, then make sure that you get involved.

#ittchat runs every Wednesday during term time from 7.00–8.00pm.

You always link with people during these chats. Follow like-minded people and enjoy the discussions that these will bring. One recommendation that I would make, to ensure that you have focused CPD from your Twitter timeline, is to only follow people that you enjoy reading information from. I interact with absolutely everybody that contacts me but only follow a few of these, so that I can really narrow down the information that I read on my timeline. Otherwise, you tend to lose Tweets from people and miss out on great information.

My 'must follows' on Twitter

This list comprises people that I find useful to connect with, along with a brief bio and their Twitter handle, so that you can follow them and see whether you are like-minded. It isn't written in any particular order and, seeing as I follow over 400 people, I will more than likely miss out some gems. Have a scan through my follow list on Twitter if you would like more than the 20 that I will give you here:

- @behaviourteach: ME! Make sure that you follow me and Tweet a picture of you and this book. I will Retweet all of the pictures that I get and this will also get you more followers from my network.

- @PookyH: Pooky Knightsmith – the director of the Charlie Waller Trust. Tweets predominantly about children and young people's mental health.

- @NatashaDevonMBE: Natasha Devon – belongs to the Self Esteem Team and Tweets about mental health.

- @SueAtkins: Sue Atkins – parenting expert. You may have seen her on BBC, ITV and Sky. She is regularly on the radio and will always support you and answer your questions.

- @jw_teach: Joe White – assistant head teacher of a school specialising in autism. He is also a principal positive behaviour support instruction. He is the host of #SpEdSC, which is a SEND slow chat that can continue through the week on different topics.

- @reachoutASC: Lynn McCann – a teacher and independent consultant for children on the autistic spectrum. She gets involved with a variety of different chats, including #behaviourchat, and also hosts. She is a great source of support on social stories.

- @MikeArmiger: Mike Armiger – he is extremely knowledgeable about LAC, mental health, trauma, attachment and behaviour. He leads on courses up and down the country and is very responsive to questions that you may have. He also has a clear way of explaining the complex area of trauma in children.

- @VPDearne: Mark Allen – vice principal working on inclusion for learning. Mark is also a Team Teach tutor. He has an interesting blog, which I would recommend, and is very reflective about his school journey, which is inspirational.

- @janeparenting2: Jane Evans – she is an independent consultant and a parenting expert. She is knowledgeable about trauma and anxiety. You will find her TED talk on YouTube.

- @Markfinnis: Mark Finnis – an expert in restorative practice. He has written many blogs and articles on the topic.

- @elsasupport: Debbie Palphreyman – provides free resources for schools that support children with social, emotional and behaviour difficulties.

- @nancygedge: Nancy Gedge – an expert in SEND. Her blog on her time in the classroom and being mum to Sam, who has Down's Syndrome, is fantastic. It won TES Blog of the year in 2015.

- @MartynReah: Martyn Reah – the man who sparked the #teacher5aday movement. He is the king of well-being!

- @pruman21: Dan Nixon – an assistant head teacher and specialist leader of education. His blogs have started being Tweeted out and are definitely well worth a read!

- @jordyjax: Jackie Ward – she has just retired and was a deputy head of a primary PRU. She is now an independent consultant for SEND and behaviour, concentrating on her mission of working with mainstream schools to prevent exclusion where possible.

- @Parkinson_best: Chris Parkinson-Best – an assistant head teacher for inclusion. He is very knowledgeable in the areas of SEMH, inclusion and behaviour. Chris also has a very active group on Facebook for teachers to discuss behaviour.

- @HilaryNunns: Hilary Nunns – an expert on ADHD, who offers a variety of courses (including online courses) for you to engage with.

- @cherrylkd: Cherryl Drabble – an expert in SEND and a specialist leader in education. She is also an assistant head and works in an outstanding-rated special school. She co-hosts #SENexchange and always responds to any queries that you have.

- @Sue_Cowley: Sue Cowley – yes, THE Sue Cowley. An expert on behaviour and author of a variety of books on behaviour management. She is very active on Twitter and will always offer her support with any questions that you may have.

- @pivotalpaul: Paul Dix – a behaviour specialist and leader of Pivotal Education. He offers a free weekly podcast, which is another source of free CPD.

Okay, so there are your first 20 follows, which will definitely enrich your timeline and pack it full of SEMH knowledge. I guarantee that you will find gems within their Tweets and, just by following them and reading these Tweets, you are increasing your subject knowledge.

TeachMeets

TeachMeets are another form of free CPD. For those who do not know, TeachMeets are simply an event where teachers meet up, discuss and network. The concept is a simple one: teachers share an idea that works for them with others. By the end of the meeting, you will have been exposed to many ideas that you may be able to implement in your classroom.

In June 2014, I ran the first TeachMeet solely focused around behaviour. Since then, it has become an annual event and, of course, you are all invited! However, you could go and run your own TeachMeet.

Decide on a date, time and place for hosting your TeachMeet. Decide on the numbers that you will be able to host and think carefully about parking spaces for the event and seating arrangements, so that it can be easily accessible for all. One thing I didn't expect was how many people would turn up who hadn't signed up previously, so be prepared for unexpected guests!

Many people advertise their event on the TeachMeet wiki page (see 'Further reading'), so that others can see the event and sign up! You can also advertise your event with a hashtag. I used #TMBehaviour for both of my events, which meant that people who were unable to attend could follow online. We even streamed content live online for those people that were following on the internet.

For my first event, I was able to secure £15,000 worth of prizes for attendees. Now, don't get me wrong, I am by no means a charmer, but I did talk to a variety of companies focused on behaviour, explaining my vision and reasons for putting on such an event. They were all keen to get on board. Some of the biggest supporters for TeachMeets are teachers who are also authors. I asked people on Twitter for support and had many responses from authors supporting me with signed copies of their books, which were very well received by the participants.

At both events, I was able to secure sponsorship so that I could provide free catering as well. I was conscious that colleagues were coming after school so wanted to make sure that they were well watered and well fed. Fish and chips for all, plus mocktails – what more could you want? Many sponsors will also support you by funding a keynote speaker to set off your event in style.

The never ending circle of behaviour

So here we are at the end of our journey together – or is it? Learning about behaviour is never finished. Why? Because the day that we finish learning about behaviour is the day that we become stagnant in our job.

If you do as you've always done, then you'll get what you've always got.

I really hope that you take control and embrace your own CPD. I hope that you do continue to develop, improve, ask questions and share strategies. Make sure that you Tweet me so I can hear all about it too!

Further reading

Books and journals

Bowlby, J. (1988), *A Secure Base: Clinical Applications of Attachment Theory.* Routledge.

Commodari, E. (2013), 'Preschool teacher attachment, school readiness and risk of learning difficulties'. *Early Childhood Research Quarterly*, 28, (1), 123–133.

Dahl, R. (1982), *The BFG.* Jonathan Cape.

Geddes, H. (2006), *Attachment in the Classroom: The Links Between Children's Early Experience, Emotional Well-being and Performance in School.* London: Worth Publishing Ltd.

Hargreaves, R. (1971–), *Mr Men* series. Egmont Books.

Rosenberg, M. B. (2003), *Nonviolent Communication: a Language of Life.* Puddle Dancer Press.

Wilson, D. and Newton, C. (2006), *Circles of Adults: A Team Approach to Problem Solving Around Challenging Behaviour and Emotional Needs.* Inclusive Solutions UK Ltd.

Blogs

Allen, M., 'Inclusion' www.vpinclusion.wordpress.com

Drabble, C. and Isherwood, M., 'SENexchangeuk' www.senexchangeuk. wordpress.com

Lawrence, T., 'Behaviour teach' www.behaviourteach.blogspot.co.uk

McGill, R. M., 'Teacher toolkit' www.teachertoolkit.co.uk

Ward, J., 'Jordyjax' www.jordyjax.wordpress.com

White, J., 'Special needs teaching and education' www.inclusiveteach.com/ author/drdig2001

Online Resources

Online Resources for this book are available at: www.bloomsbury.com/ primary-practical-behaviour-management

Other online sources

Childhood Bereavement Network, 'National statistics' <http://www.childhoodbereavementnetwork.org.uk/research/key-statistics.aspx>

Department for Education (2013), 'Behaviour and guidance in schools' <https://www.gov.uk/government/publications/behaviour-and-discipline-in-schools>

Department for Education (2016), 'Counselling in schools: a blueprint for the future' <https://www.gov.uk/government/uploads/system/uploads/attachment_data/file/497825/Counselling_in_schools.pdf>

Department for Education and Department of Health (2014), 'SEND code of practice: 0 to 25 years' <https://www.gov.uk/government/publications/send-code-of-practice-0-to-25>

'Lego Therapy' <http://www.legotherapy.com/links/>

National Institute of Mental Health, 'Any disorder among children' <https://www.nimh.nih.gov/health/statistics/prevalence/any-disorder-among-children.shtml>

NHS Choices, 'Five steps to mental well-being' <http://www.nhs.uk/Conditions/stress-anxiety-depression/Pages/improve-mental-wellbeing.aspx>

Oxford University Press, 'English: Oxford Living Dictionaries' <http://www.oxforddictionaries.com/definition/english/behaviour>

Reah, M. (2016), 'UKEdMag: Teacher 5-a-day' (*UKEdChat*) <http://ukedchat.com/2016/08/30/ukedmag-teacher-5-a-day-by-martynreah-teacher5aday/>

Standards and Testing Agency (2016), 'Rochford Review: final report' <https://www.gov.uk/government/publications/rochford-review-final-report>https://www.gov.uk/government/publications/rochford-review-final-report>

'TeachMeet' <http://teachmeet.pbworks.com/w/page/19975349/FrontPage>

TES (2015), '100 fiction books all children should read before leaving primary school – according to teachers' <https://www.tes.com/news/school-news/breaking-news/100-fiction-books-all-children-should-read-leaving-primary-school-%E2%80%93>

The Nurture Group Network, 'The Boxall Profile' <https://nurturegroups.org/introducing-nurture/boxall-profile>

Youthinmind, 'SDQ: Information for researchers and professionals about the Strengths & Difficulties Questionnaires' <http://www.sdqinfo.org/>

Index